and now . . .

NEXT DOOR

and

DOWN THE FREEWAY

DEVELOPING A MISSIONAL STRATEGY FOR USA/CANADA

D1022768

NEIL B. WISEMAN
editor

Beacon Hill Press of Kansas City
Kansas City, Missouri

Copyright 2001
by Beacon Hill Press of Kansas City

ISBN 083-411-9080

Cover Design: Michael Walsh

All Scripture quotations not otherwise designated are from the *Holy Bible, New International Version®* (NIV®). Copyright © 1973, 1978, 1984 by International Bible Society. Used by permission of Zondervan Publishing House. All rights reserved.

Permission to quote from the following additional copyrighted versions of the Bible is acknowledged with appreciation:

The *New American Standard Bible®* (NASB®), © copyright The Lockman Foundation 1960, 1962, 1963, 1968, 1971, 1972, 1973, 1975, 1977, 1995.

The Message (TM). Copyright © 1993. Used by permission of NavPress Publishing Group.

10   9   8   7   6   5   4   3   2   1

Contents

Proclamation

We must see the United States and
Canada as part of the global mission
field as never before, and we must
commit ourselves to this ministry.
Cultural diversity, human need,
and urbanization converge as
the cutting-edge issues that will
increasingly demand a response
from the church in its
evangelistic mission.

—Board of General Superintendents
Annual report to General Board
February 1997

Core Value

Our Mission of Compassion and Evangelism

AS PEOPLE who are consecrated to God, we share His love for the lost and His compassion for the poor and broken. The Great Commandment and the Great Commission move us to engage the world in evangelism, compassion, and justice. To this end we are committed to inviting people to faith, to caring for those in need, to standing against injustice and with the oppressed, to working to protect and preserve the resources of God's creation, and to including in our fellowship all who will call upon the name of the Lord.

Through its mission in the world, the church demonstrates the love of God. The story of the Bible is the story of God reconciling the world to himself, ultimately through Christ Jesus (2 Cor. 5:16-21). The church is sent into the world to participate with God in this ministry of love and reconciliation through evangelism, compassion, and justice.

—Core Values Booklet

A Heart Message
to Frontline Personnel

A GOD-INSPIRED renewed passion for mission in the United States and Canada is underway across the Church of the Nazarene. Some call it a holy revolution of vision and focus. From many sources—from the grass roots to districts to educational institutions to the Board of General Superintendents—a simultaneous commitment and conviction have sprung up that the same missionary zeal Nazarenes have always had for unreached people in distant lands is now needed in the United States and Canada.

The chapters of this book are abridged from messages presented to various Nazarene groups. Each contributor is a faithful member of our Nazarene family, and each believes passionately in a magnificently productive future for our church, providing every component of the church becomes militantly missional. Through these pages the common thread is that our mission fields are everywhere—next door, in the next town, and around the world.

The contemporary call is for us to lead in thinking and acting like missionaries and to challenge our congregations to do the same. Millions who do not know Christ—especially nearby secularists, recent immigrants, and your next-door neighbors—need to hear about Him from your missionally motivated commitment.

Look into your heart for the energy to start.

—*Neil B. Wiseman, editor*

WE MUST BECOME A MISSIONAL PEOPLE

Bill M. Sullivan

IT IS REALLY SOMETHING to have lived through the change of a millennium—and even the turn of a century. But without realizing it, we have also lived through the end of an era. We have seen America go from over 200 years of a basically Christian culture to a non-Christian culture that rejects the foundational principles of Christianity.

High-visibility Christian leaders are in scarce supply. Mother Teresa is gone. C. S. Lewis is gone. Billy Graham is set to conclude his ministry.

We have been blessed with great leaders in the past—not only clergy but also lay leaders. They have served us well in the era of Christendom. We owe them a great debt of gratitude.

The question now is this: What kind of leaders are needed in the 21st century?

In the 20th century, we were a *sending* church. Our leaders led the way in sending missionaries around the world. But in the 21st century, we must be a *sent* church, because the mission field is all around us—right here in North America.

Kennon Callahan, a prominent contemporary Christian thinker, believes, "The day of the churched culture is gone, the day of the mission field has come; the day of the institu-

tional church is past, the day of the mission outpost has arrived; the day of the professional minister is over, the day of
the missional pastor is here."

David McKenna, former president of Asbury Theological
Seminary and a highly visible leader among Wesleyans, has
said the present situation in North America requires that
"every church must be a mission station, and every Christian
a missionary."

If the Church of the Nazarene is to be a spiritually impacting denomination in the 21st century, it must get in step
with the new yet very old concept of what it means to be
missional. We must become missional people.

You probably wonder what I mean by *missional,* so allow me to characterize missional people briefly.

*In order to become missional people, we must embrace a
strong faith in God.* You may say, "We already have faith in
God. That doesn't help define *missional."*

Remember that Jesus said, "When the Son of Man
comes, will he find faith on the earth?" (Luke 18:8). We are
talking about more than a casual faith. A timid, acquiescing,
capitulating faith will not support a passionate mission to
win people to Christ and the Church.

Faith in the Creative Power of God

Missional people have a strong faith in God as the Creator. They confidently sing,

> *This is my Father's world,*
> *And to my list'ning ears*
> *All nature sings, and round me rings*
> *The music of the spheres.*
> —Maltbie D. Babcock

Missional people maintain a strong commitment to
God's control and intervention in the world. The confidence
of missional people is not undermined by naturalistic asser-
tions from the scientific community.

We're not talking about being naive or blind to apparent

facts. We're asserting that faith transcends the unknown and the unknowable.

Those who do not believe in the God of the Bible try to make God in the image of humanity. They want to reduce God to human comparisons. But listen to what God says: "My thoughts are not your thoughts, neither are your ways my ways. As the heavens are higher than the earth, so are my ways higher than your ways and my thoughts than your thoughts" (Isa. 55:8-9).

Too many Christians are fearful that anthropology and astronomy are closing in on the idea of the existence of a Supreme Being, whom we in the Western world call the God of the Bible. Don't worry about that happening. Things aren't always what they seem to be.

I'm reminded of a story about two natural gas company servicemen who were out checking meters in a suburban neighborhood. They parked their truck at one end of the alley and worked their way to the other end. At the last house, a woman looking out her kitchen window watched the two men as they checked her gas meter. Finishing the check, one of the servicemen challenged the other to a foot race back down the alley to the truck. As they came running up to the truck, they realized that the lady from the last house was huffing and puffing right behind them. They stopped and asked her what was wrong. Gasping for breath, she said, "When I saw two gas men running full speed away from my house, I figured I'd better run too!"

Again, things aren't always what they appear to be. There's a lot to be learned about the universe yet, and in the end it may turn out to be quite different than earlier research has indicated.

Faith in the Redemptive Power of God

If we want to be missional people, our faith in God must embrace not only His creative power but also His redemptive purposes. He is the Creator God, but He is also the Redeemer God. He wants to restore people to their rightful relationship with Him.

Years ago I heard Frank Laubach, a great Christian remembered for his "Each One Teach One" concept, say, "We can't be right with God until we are right with God's problem, and God's problem is that people are estranged from God."

I can still hear thundering in my soul the words of the late great missiologist Donald McGavran: "God wants the lost found!"

Missional people accept the fact that God wants His followers to find the lost. They know God works in this world, but they know God expects them to work also.

Faith in the Redemptive Work of Believers

Missional people accept the Great Commission as God's directive to them. They know He has already told them what to do. They are not waiting for further instructions. The evangelization of the world waits not on the readiness of God but on the obedience of Christians.

We hear a lot of people today say, "Join God where He's working." That sounds nice, but it isn't really biblical. For the Great Commission tells us to go, and *God* will join *us* wherever we work" because He has promised, "Surely I am with you always, to the very end of the age" (Matt. 28:20).

The Church of the Nazarene will be a spiritually influential denomination in the 21st century, because its members determine that they will be missional people. And missional people embrace a strong faith in the Creator and Redeemer God.

In order to become missional people, we must be open to the call and leading of God. One of the interesting aspects of great movings of the Holy Spirit is the emergence of new ministries and surprising leaders for those ministries. God keeps surprising us with creativity and newness.

Consider God's Call to All

Missional people receive and accept a call from God that may not be only to the ordained clergy. This is a very delicate area that theologians and professional clergy discuss with great passion. God keeps doing His work through people who listen and obey.

We know the New Testament does not make a distinction between the clergy and the laity. Yet the Old Testament priest and prophet roles linger in the thinking of New Testament churches.

Organizationally, the clergy has been a functional convenience. And no one denies the value of an effective leader—clergy or lay. Yet it appears that God is calling laypersons to significant involvement in the work of the Church that's not necessarily a call to preach. Whether this is really different than it has always been I cannot say. I only know that missional people today are open to the call and leading of God in their lives.

Some people may find such changes difficult to accept. I recently saw a bumper sticker that read, "The Ship Sank. Get Over It!" Someone needs to print a bumper sticker for Christians that says, "You Don't Have God Figured Out. Get Used to It!" God isn't obligated to work according to our bylaws and organizational structures. And He doesn't.

A friend of mine told me about visiting his mother at their district camp meeting. After the service, his mother declared with a tinge of disgust or perhaps frustration in her voice, "This is not the Church of the Nazarene I joined!" A while back I made a list of 20 things that had changed in the Church of the Nazarene in the past 25 years. And I can understand why my friend's mother felt as though she was in a different church from the one she had joined years earlier.

If we think the Church of the Nazarene has changed, it is minimal to what has changed in the church world generally. To use the old term "mainline" when referring to traditional denominations is really an oxymoron. For they are not mainline anymore. They no longer control religion in America. In fact, denominations of any kind no longer control religion in America. Parachurch organizations and large local churches are the dominant forces in American religion today.

Why should we be surprised that God is doing a new thing in the Church today? He is calling people to new forms of evangelism and ministry.

It doesn't make much difference, because religion in North America is seriously compromised and weak. Research reveals minimal or no difference between the lifestyles of Christians and non-Christians. Consequently, non-Christians see no reason why they should become Christians. Why attend all those meetings when there is no difference?

Why should we be surprised that God is doing a new thing in the Church today? He is calling people to new forms of evangelism and ministry, and it's blowing right past most clergy and not a few laypersons.

But missional people see it—because they are open to the call and leading of God in new and surprising ways.

I don't know how you feel about it, but be prepared for a dramatic increase in the number of women clergy—and lay leaders who give primary leadership to local churches. God is not limited to our concepts of church and ministry. He's calling a corps of missional people who will respond to His call and leading in their lives.

I want to complete my characterization of missional people with a phrase borrowed from modern management literature. It is as old as the Great Commission: Think globally and act locally.

In order to be missional people, we must think globally and act locally. Jesus said the goal is to win the entire world—but start where you are. Begin in Jerusalem. Move out to Judea and Samaria, then on to the ends of the earth.

Our problem today is that we began locally and then progressed globally. But while we were evangelizing globally, the local situation changed dramatically. The United States, which was once widely considered a Christian nation, has become significantly non-Christian and even anti-Christian. Now other nations are sending missionaries to the United States and are challenging our understanding of the term "mission field." We have always thought that the mission field was "over there." But it's right here where we live and work. It's next door and down the street and across town.

Confounding us even more is the declaration of the Board of General Superintendents that the United States is a mission field. If the United States is a mission field, then what is Africa?

There is a rather interesting debate going on in the church right now about *who is a missionary*. It's kind of like the debate we have had for years about *who is a minister*. I don't want to oversimplify these issues, but it is interesting to note that it is the professional missionary and the professional minister who are most passionate about the definitions.

When I was a teenager, I remember hearing my pastor say, "If you're not a missionary at home, you're not prepared to be a missionary abroad." He questioned the sincerity of a person who professed a call to the mission field in Africa but wouldn't share the love of Jesus with an African-American who lived a few blocks away.

My pastor had it exactly right—global starts as local. In an ultimate sense, there will be no global missions if we don't have strong, effective local mission.

Acting locally involves a commitment to develop sensitivity to needs heretofore unobserved. It displays a willingness to seize opportunities that open up or even to push open some apparently closed doors. And it readily shoulders the responsibilities entailed in completing the task that follows.

I could give specific examples, but they might misdirect you. The important fact is missional people look for needs and opportunities to share God's love with people who do not know Him.

Missional people are not just verbal witnesses who talk about faith. Increasingly in North America, people don't care what we think or believe—instead, they're interested in knowing what we do and who we are. They want to know about integrity and authenticity. Verbal witness is necessary, but it's not enough.

Billy Graham tells of witnessing to a man about becoming a Christian. The man listened politely and then replied, "I'll become a Christian when I see one." Verbal witness is just not enough—even for Billy Graham.

"Missional" Starts with Who We Are Inside

My appeal is that we give serious consideration to all those unreasonable statements in Jesus' Sermon on the Mount. I mean basic principles like

"Love your enemies and pray for those who persecute you" (Matt. 5:44).

"If someone forces you to go one mile, go with him two miles" (v. 41).

"Do not judge. . . . Why do you look at the speck of sawdust in your brother's eye and pay no attention to the plank in your own eye?" (7:1, 3)

"Do not store up for yourself treasures on earth. . . . But store up for yourselves treasures in heaven" (6:19-20).

"Do not worry about your life, what you will eat or drink; or about your body, what you will wear. Is not life more important than food, and the body more important than clothes?" (v. 25).

Renowned pollster George Gallup has studied religion in North America extensively for decades. He sounds like a prophet when he calls attention to the impact of the religious knowledge gap, radical individualism, and nominalism in North American churches. "Belief without practice," he says, "is producing an indifferent population."

When we live the Sermon on the Mount, people will start listening to what we say. It was that way in the Early Church, and it will be that way in the 21st century.

Sociologist Rodney Stark wrote a book titled *The Rise of Christianity: How the Obscure, Marginal Jesus Movement Became the Dominant Religious Force in the Western World in a Few Centuries*. Stark describes how people, living out the basic principles of their faith, won the Western world to Christianity.

One example stands out.

When plagues struck cities in early centuries, the death toll was often enormous—sometimes killing one-third to one-half of the population. Those who were able fled the cities until the epidemic was over. However, Christians did not desert the plague-ridden cities. They remained and cared for the sick—not only their fellow Christians but their pagan neighbors as well. They saw this as the obvious response to their Lord's command to love their enemies. Many of the sick survived simply because they were given care rather than being abandoned. When the plague abated and people returned to the cities, they found pagan friends with a new attitude of openness toward Christianity.

Please understand—they didn't go looking for a plague, but when it came, they had the courage to respond in keeping with their Lord's commands.

Missional people are not just those who travel around the world—and God bless those who do.

Missional people are followers of Christ who firmly believe in His coming kingdom and live their lives to share His love and hope with everyone—whether they live just down the street or around the world.

Americans are reeling emotionally from daily life in a society traumatized by too much violence, too many divided families, and too little job security. The pain and isolation caused by reliance on material things and on human resources alone has grown unbearable.

—Claude E. Payne
Reclaiming the Great Commission

2

WE ARE LIVING IN A MISSION FIELD

Tom Nees

A WALK AROUND the once middle- to upper-middle-class neighborhood surrounding Los Angeles First Church of the Nazarene tells the story. Many storefront businesses have signs in languages other than English. Foreign-speaking, immigrant-working people of apparently limited financial means crowd the streets. Buddhist temples and Muslim mosques stand alongside Christian churches. This doesn't look like the America it once was. To many Nazarenes, it looks like some foreign, non-Christian country. Any way you view this changing scene, it is now a mission field.

You don't have to leave Kansas City to be among Cambodians, Koreans, Hispanics, and Samoans. With 1 million people from over 100 world areas immigrating to the United States annually, a few years from now even the most traditional United States towns will become multicultural. Many if not most local congregations will find themselves surrounded by changing neighborhoods. Without leaving town, they will have opportunity to fulfill the missional mandate of Acts 1:8—"witnesses in Jerusalem, and in all Judea and Samaria, and to the ends of the earth." If missionary work means communicating the gospel across the barriers of language and culture, then indeed North America became a mission field long before church officials declared it so, and it is becoming more so every day.

A Radically New Way of Doing Ministry

In 1997 the Board of General Superintendents challenged the church to recognize that, along with the rest of the world, the United States and Canada are mission fields. In declaring that our countries are mission fields, they are leading the church to the cutting edge of human need and Kingdom opportunity. That declaration has the potential of radically changing the way ministry is done in the United States and Canada. If fully understood, it will dramatically change the way we look at the world and every aspect of a local church's ministry.

In the 1997 District Superintendents' Leadership Development Program sponsored by the Evangelism and Church Growth Division, Paul Dietterrich, director of theological research at the Center for Parish Development in Chicago, said that the declaration by our leaders is one of the most progressive and significant statements on the mission of the church to come from any denomination.

Leaders from Nazarene Mission Fields

It would be a mistake, however, to think of the United States and Canada as a mission field simply because of the annual influx of 1 million immigrants from over 100 world areas. Admittedly, immigrants and refugees are changing the face of our countries as well as our churches, contributing to religious pluralism. Yet many of those immigrating from Latin America, Asia, and Africa are more passionate about sharing the gospel than native-born Christians.

Hundreds of Nazarenes have been among the tens of thousands of immigrants who have come to the United States and Canada in recent years.

When pioneer Nazarene missionaries opened work in countries like Guatemala, Korea, and Haiti, never in their wildest imagination could they have anticipated that the human fruit of their labors would include a generation of missional leaders in the United States and Canada. The rapid growth of the immigrant church—the fastest growing segment of the church during the past decade—is the direct result of the success of Nazarene missions around the world.

Hundreds of Nazarenes have been among the tens of thousands of immigrants who have come to the United States and Canada in recent years. Many of them are dedicated leaders trained by missionaries who now feel called by God to be missionaries in their new world. Ninety percent of the Korean, Hispanic, and Haitian pastors in the United States and Canada were converted, trained, and ordained on foreign mission fields.

Though Nazarene immigrants number less than 10 percent of the church in the United States and Canada, they have been starting fully half of the new churches in recent years.

Like Immigrants, Secular People Need Christ

Driving this new definition of North America as a mission field is the realization that in the United States and Canada and other Western countries, secular culture is not conducive to vital Christian faith. Christianity is now growing fastest in non-Western countries, where the majority of Christians now live.

In 1996, Kennon Callahan spoke to Nazarene district superintendents in San Francisco, repeating what he has written: "The day of the professional minister is over. The day of the missionary has come. . . . The day of the churched culture is over. The day of the mission field has come. . . . The day of the local church is over. The day of the mission outpost has come." And the outpost is your community.

Not too long ago I was preaching a Sunday morning

message to an older, established congregation on "The Marks of a Missional Church." I asked a question that I intended to answer. "What would be different about this congregation if it took this new definition of mission seriously?" A woman stood to her feet and responded in a voice loud enough for the entire congregation to hear: "Well, we sure wouldn't be sitting here," she said.

This lady recognized that a missional church would be doing something more, or at least different, on Sunday morning. If her neighborhood is a mission field and her church is to be on a mission, some things would have to change.

Church Is Marginalized in Modernity

Alan Roxburgh, a pastor in Vancouver, British Columbia, and a faculty member at Regent College, writes, "Congregations must now learn how to live the gospel as a distinct people who are no longer at the cultural center. Unless leaders recognize and understand the extent to which they and congregations have been marginalized in modernity, they will not meaningfully shape the directions of congregational life for a missionary engagement" (Douglas Hall, *The End of Christendom and the Future of Christianity*).

Along with other writers, such as Douglas Hall in *The End of Christendom and the Future of Christianity,* Roxburgh suggests that "the fourth and twentieth centuries form bookends marking transition points in the history of the church." According to this view, Western culture is in a transition from 16 centuries of Christendom during which Christianity was the official religion of the state churches of Europe and the cultural or civic religion of the United States.

We are beginning to recognize that Western cultural values, in spite of the remaining symbols of Christendom, are often alien, if not outright hostile, to the gospel. We cannot look to our pagan culture with its religious pluralism and secularism for help in developing a missional church.

Declaring the United States and Canada as a new mission field is tantamount to admitting that North America with all its Christian traditions and churches may be as unchristian as the "mission fields" in countries thought in the past to be unfamiliar with, if not unfriendly to, the gospel.

Why Rethink Missions in the United States and Canada?

The church in a mission field will need to rethink the way it does ministry. Sending and supporting missionaries without doing missionary work at home will no longer attract the support of a generation looking for congregations on a mission in their own neighborhoods that are becoming as diverse and needy as the global community.

To effectively communicate the gospel in the 21st century will take a degree of flexibility, openness, and the ability to do cultural exegesis formerly thought to be the special calling of missionaries. Often this will require American missional leaders as well as church members to be aware of and comfortable with several cultures at once.

Missionary work still means being sent from one culture to another even if that means going across town or across the street. During our missionary recruiting services we still sing, "It may not be on the mountain's height, / Or over the stormy sea; . . . / My Lord will have need of me." It may be in our own backyard.

Special Assignment Missionaries Cannot Do It All

With this as background, the World Mission Division and the Evangelism and Church Growth Division have collaborated to appoint missionaries to the United States and Canada. The strategy is to concentrate on minority groups and urban areas where there are concentrations of under-evangelized neighborhoods and unreached people groups. Specialized assigned missionaries are being appointed to multidistrict areas where there is agreement to develop and implement common mission strategies.

A major challenge is to communicate to the church in the United States and Canada that the appointment of missionaries is one part, if not a small part, of a much larger missional strategy—and not the strategy itself. Twenty-first-century missions and evangelism are developing as a comprehensive strategy to develop missional leaders and missional churches in every city, in every neighborhood, among all people groups.

NewStart Provides Aggressive Missional Strategy

The NewStart program—"starting strong new churches the right way"—is an aggressive plan encouraging congregations to become missional by sponsoring new churches. Churches of all sizes in small towns, suburbs, and central cities have begun to sponsor new congregations, sometimes within their own buildings. More than 200 churches now share their buildings with one or more other language minority groups.

Several districts have appointed their own specially assigned missionaries.

Appointing a few missionaries here and there will not in itself make much difference unless these missionaries serve as facilitators of missional objectives designed and owned by districts and local congregations. Several districts have appointed their own specially assigned missionaries. Local congregations may also support and send their own missional leaders.

Missionaries in the 21st century will likely include a variety of local, district, and general church-supported laity, as well as clergy leaders, all of them on a mission to win people to Christ and the church.

Facilitating this missionary endorsement and appointment process requires a close working relationship with the World Mission Division (the sending agency of the Church of the Nazarene), the Evangelism and Church Growth Division (where missional strategies for the United States and Canada are developed), and with each district and potentially every congregation. All this requires a new way of implementing the mission of the church.

The world is no longer divided between the sending and receiving nations. The global village, where countries are inextricably intertwined by commerce and communication, is one large mission field. If the church in the United States and Canada is to keep pace with the growth of the church in other world areas, then some of the missional strategies it has supported around the world need to find their place here.

In the late 1980s José Alfaro, a Guatemalan immigrant pastor and product of Nazarene missions, came to the United States. During the Thrust to the Cities program, he started a Spanish-speaking church in Chicago. In the short years since, he has built one of our largest Hispanic churches while at the same time training others to start 10 other churches, including the first Russian Nazarene congregation in Chicago.

Using strategies he knew well in Guatemala, he has established a mission training center in his own church. When a leader is prepared to start a new church, he or she is given a core group of members from the parent church. Pastor Alfaro continues to serve as mentor to the new pastors and supporter of the new congregations.

Missions will be directed by Nazarenes who have sent and supported missionaries abroad and those like Rev. Alfaro who have come to their adopted homeland on a mission to spread the gospel.

The majority English-speaking white population is no

less in need than the millions of minorities who will become the majority by mid-century.

You Live on a Mission Field

We are living in a new mission field that could become the place of renewal for missional leaders and missional churches. Historically, within the Wesleyan-Holiness tradition, our message has been our mission. Following John Wesley, our mission has been to "spread Scriptural holiness throughout the land and reform the nation."

The Board of General Superintendents has not only redefined our mission by declaring the United States and Canada as a mission field but also recently reframed our beliefs and core values with the theme "Holiness—The Message of Hope."

The new missional strategy will be driven by laity, pastors, evangelists, educators, missionaries, administrators, and denominational leaders on a common mission with a message of hope.

In churches, on districts, among students, in conventions and assemblies, the call has gone out for everyone to be on a mission of hope for a hurting world.

Sound the challenge in your congregation. Join the revolution. This cause will change you forever. And the Lord will use your missional efforts to transform previously unreached people.

3

"MISSIONAL" IS
IN OUR BONES

Ron Benefiel

NOT LONG AGO I found myself fully engaged in a probing
discussion about the mission of the church with Clarence
Kinzler, Nazarene district superintendent of the Northern
California District. We talked about the rediscovery of our
message in the proclamation of holiness as Christlikeness.
And we talked about how crucial it is for us to rediscover
our calling to be a people of compassion and justice without
losing our commitment to evangelism. As we neared the end
of our discussion, Clari said, "Compassionate ministries
come naturally for us. Way down deep, it's part of who we
are. It's in our bones!"

As I thought some more about the discussion, I had a
glimpse of what I think our church can be and what I hope
it is becoming—a movement of Holiness people who are
radically and fully committed to God, to one another, and to
the mission of the church. A church drawn by the heart of
God into the midst of a broken world. A people who, in
obedience and joy, witness to the coming Kingdom through
their love for one another and their love for the poor, the
lost, and the broken of the world. A people who take both
the Great Commission and the Great Commandment seriously. The Church of the Nazarene—a people of evangelism,
compassion, justice. *It's in our bones!*

I BELIEVE GOD RAISED UP
THE CHURCH OF THE NAZARENE

Perhaps the greatest privilege of my life was to serve as pastor of the First Church of the Nazarene in Los Angeles. It is a church with a glorious heritage—founded in 1895 by Phineas F. Bresee, the first congregation anywhere to bear the name Church of the Nazarene. Over the years that I was there, I learned a lot about the early days of the church with all of its struggles and victories. I gained a great respect for the people who laid the foundation upon which we all have built. Those beginning days of the church were characterized by a spirit of spontaneous revival with wonderful stories of people being radically transformed by the grace of God. They were days when the presence of the Lord was so real and vital that they called their place of worship the Glory Barn. The church began with a little over 100 charter members and numbered over 1,000 a decade later.

In the church basement is a very unusual room, specifically set aside to house the church archives. The contents of this room tell the story of God raising up a new church under the leadership of Dr. Bresee. It really is an interesting place, full of old bulletins, pictures, documents, furniture, and artifacts from days gone by, all carefully and neatly displayed and all serving as reminders of a great spiritual revival of a century ago. All the pulpits used over the 106-year life of the church, from the Glory Barn on, are stored there, along with Dr. Bresee's desk, chairs from the platform of Dr. Bresee's church at 6th and Wall, and an antique pump organ they used back then for street meetings. Just walking into the room makes me feel a little wiser and a whole lot older.

So much has changed in Los Angeles over the years that it's a bit difficult at times to picture the events depicted in the archives actually occurring on the streets of our city. One thing is very clear, however: something quite extraordinary was happening in Los Angeles 106 years ago. God was doing something unique and powerful in the lives of the people who called themselves Nazarenes.

The focal point of the revival was on the person and work of the Holy Spirit in the lives of believers. To miss this would be to miss the driving force behind the power-filled fledgling church. The people who came to the Glory Barn experienced the glory of God poured out upon them. They discovered in their daily lives that as they surrendered themselves to God, He did a work of power and purity in them that utterly transformed their lives. In 1905 Dr. Bresee stated in a sermon later reprinted in the December edition of the *Nazarene Messenger*, "There is one thing primarily necessary—to be filled with the power of the Spirit. . . . This is the first great necessity. Without it—nothing; with it—all things."

Transforming Grace for Everyone

Now this is really what I want you to hear. Early Nazarenes believed that what God was doing in their lives He could do in the life of anyone. They preached and believed that there was no one who was beyond the reach of God—no one who could not be saved, no one who was so lost that he or she could not be found. The rich and the poor, the revivalist and the secularist, the immigrant, migrant, and native all found that the gospel was for them.

In a sermon appearing in the July 1903 *Nazarene Messenger*, Dr. Bresee wrote, "The imparted power by the Holy Ghost thrills and fills and burns in living testimony. . . . Victory and glory are assured. . . . Drunkards and harlots, the unlettered, every humble, earnest, longing soul can know the power of God to save to the uttermost." It is apparent that early Nazarenes genuinely and earnestly believed in the transforming power of the grace of God. They were optimistic in their engagement of the world around them because they were optimistic about grace.

Actually, there may even be a hint of all this in the name Nazarene. I remember growing up in the church thinking often that the choice of the name, Church of the Nazarene, seemed a bit unfortunate. I felt that I was forever explaining to people that the Church of the Nazarene was, in fact, Christian and not some cult group. In responding to the inquiries, I would patiently explain that Jesus was a Nazarene (from Nazareth), and therefore Church of the Nazarene was simply another way of saying Church of Jesus. At times it seemed to me that it would have been simpler if the founding fathers would have given us a name that more readily identified us with mainstream Christianity. God's Church would have been just fine with me.

I also remember my pastor father emphasizing to the faithful that technically we were not "the Nazarene Church," as many often referred to us, but the Church of the Nazarene. He would explain that "the Nazarene Church" didn't really mean anything, but that the Church of the Nazarene was another way of saying that we were followers of Jesus Christ. It made sense to me. After all, Matt. 2:23 clearly stated that Jesus was raised in Nazareth, "This was to fulfill what was spoken through the prophets: 'He shall be called a Nazarene'" (NASB).

I later discovered that there was one little hitch in all of this. Apparently in Jesus' day, to be from Nazareth was to be looked down upon ("Can any good thing come out of Nazareth?"). To be a Nazarene was to be despised. To be called a Nazarene was something close to being called a bad word.

At this point, I'm not sure I'm feeling any better about being part of a church named Church of the Nazarene. Church of the Despised is not exactly an enticing name when it comes to inviting my friends. Here I spent all this time growing up trying to explain what a Nazarene was in a way that would make it sound respectable. And now to discover that perhaps it's not such a respectable name after all. Surely our founding fathers must have made a mistake. Did they really know what they were doing when they labeled us for life Church of the Nazarene—Church of the Despised?

Now this part may surprise you a bit. Apparently they knew exactly what they were doing when they came up with our name. The one who originally submitted it was J. P. Widney, former president of the University of Southern California and cofounder of the Church of the Nazarene in Los Angeles. In *Called unto Holiness*, Timothy Smith notes, "The word 'Nazarene' had come to him one morning at daybreak after a whole night of prayer. . . . it was the name which Jesus used of himself, 'the name which was used in derision of Him by His enemies,' the name which above all others linked Him to 'the great toiling, sorrowing heart of the world. It is Jesus, Jesus of Nazareth, to whom the world in its misery and despair turns, that it may have hope.'"

So, there you have it. There's no escaping it. When it comes right down to it, all of us who call ourselves Nazarenes are by intention and name part of the Church of the Despised.

I Like Our Name

The more I think about this, the more it begins to make sense to me. Jesus' mission was not to gain recognition and prestige, but to do the work the Father had sent Him to do in telling the whole world of the love of God. Jesus, as a Nazarene, spent much of His time loving and caring for those who were the dispossessed of His world—the poor, the sick, Samaritans, the leprous, tax collectors—the down-and-outs of His world.

It occurs to me that Nazarene is not just our name—it is part of our calling as well. Our mission is not necessarily to enter the ranks of the prestigious, but to carry out the call of God ministering to *all* who are in need. Maybe this is one of the very few times my dad was wrong. Maybe we *are* to be the Nazarene Church, the place where the Nazarenes of our world know they are welcome. (Or maybe you could simply say that we are a church of Nazarenes.) In the same way that Jesus cared for the lost of the world, perhaps the stigmatized and disregarded of our world are the ones God has especially called us to love and care for. Could it be, after all, that part of the reason God raised up the Church of the Nazarene is to be a church in which *everyone* and *anyone* truly and genuinely is welcomed and embraced and loved?

In the September 1901 *Nazarene Messenger*, Dr. Bresee wrote, "The evidence of the presence of Jesus in our midst is that we bear the gospel, primarily to the poor." In a January 1902 issue, he wrote, "We can get along without rich people, but not without preaching the gospel to the poor." And in an October 1898 *Nazarene Messenger* article, he wrote, "The gospel comes to a multitude without money and without price, and the poorest of the poor are entitled to a front seat at the Church of the Nazarene, the only condition being that they come early enough to get there."

Los Angeles has changed a lot over the years. Even the faces of the dispossessed are different now than they were over 100 years ago—homeless families, ex-cons, undocumented immigrants, people with AIDS. But I want to suggest that God's call on the people called Nazarenes has not changed. For it is still true, perhaps more than ever, that people in our neighborhoods need the transforming work of God in their lives. They need to hear the Good News, be forgiven of their sins, and be filled with the cleansing power of the Holy Spirit. And it is still true, as true as ever, that the good news is literally for everyone, including the poor. God continues to call us to be a church where everyone is welcome—a church for *all* people.

A MISSION TO THE NEIGHBORHOOD AS WELL AS THE WORLD

Those early days were days when ministry to and among the lost, the poor, and the broken was right at the heart of the mission of the church. New congregations and cross-cultural missions were started in surrounding neighborhoods. Not only in Los Angeles but across the nation, the people called Nazarenes were people who became known for their care for individuals in need. Rest cottages (homes for unwed mothers), orphanages, and rescue missions sprouted up all over the Nazarene map. Articles championing social justice and discussing the plight of the poor appeared in the *Herald of Holiness*. To minister among the poor was central to the missional identity of the church.

The question is, *Are we still a people with a mission?* Is it only sentimentalism to look back to those early days with idealistic stars in our eyes, or is the mission that God impressed upon our early leaders still a mission for the church today? The point of my writing to you is to assert as strongly and urgently as I can my conviction that just as God raised up the Church of the Nazarene and called her to a Kingdom mission as the world entered the 20th century, God calls us again to Kingdom mission as we enter the 21st century. The days of being a missional people are not past. The call for us to be the people of God in mission is upon us today.

REENERGIZING OUR MISSION FOR OUR TIMES

• **A radical commitment to follow Jesus.** If we are to be a missional people, the first commitment we must be willing to make is to be a Holiness people—set apart unto God—committed wholly to Christ and to Christlikeness. We must be a people who learn what it means to abide in Christ, so that God's priorities and values increasingly become our own and the things that break the heart of God break ours as well. This is not new. We Nazarenes know this as God's call. And we know that it is possible only by God's grace.

• **An intentional commitment to one another in Kingdom community.** It is not news that we live in an individualistic, consumerist world. But when individualism and consumerism invade the church, we have a problem. Consumerism in the church influences us to offer more and have it cost less than the competition, that's basic consumer economics. In the church, this is a form of cheap grace. A consumer orientation in the church is preference oriented in which the driving question for our involvement is, "Does this church meet my needs and the needs of my family?" If we allow this mentality to flourish in the church, it will destroy Christian community and ultimately destroy the ability of the church to be missional. To be a Christian community in mission requires *commitment.* Consumerism thrives on *convenience* and *personal preference.* A church organized around self-interest and satisfaction of personal need will not have the depth or stamina to call its people to be love-committed to one another.

We must be love-committed to one another, living our lives together out of the center of a Kingdom community.

And if we are truly going to be the Church of Jesus Christ, we must be love-committed to one another, living our lives together out of the center of a Kingdom community. When this happens, Christ, the Christian community, and the work of the church become our corporate passion around which the rest of life is organized. Vocation and recreation move to the margins rather than being the centerpiece of our lives. Family life is not removed from the church but rather is lived in and around the center of Christian community. As a Kingdom community, people in the world should be able to look at us—a Holiness community—and see what the kingdom of God is all about. In our world today, this is countercultural. It is possible only by the grace of God.

• **A renewed commitment to the mission of the church.** In a sinful, hurting, scary world, our natural tendency is to flee. Self-protection and protection of our family become our highest concerns. Our tendency is to move away from the pain, misery, and real danger of the world. But to follow Jesus is to follow Him right into the middle of the fray. The mission of the church is, at its heart, incarnational. Rather than trying to escape or flee, the call to follow Christ moves us as a Christian community toward those in need, those in pain, and those suffering tragedy.

We have a great history of being a sending church—sending missionaries to far-off places to preach the Good News. This has been one of our great strengths. But if we are going to follow the call of God to be a church in Kingdom mission, we will *all* need to take on a missionary spirit. We will need to move from being a sending church to being a sent church, all of us together, following Christ into the middle of a sinful, broken world. This is countercultural. It is possible only by the grace of God.

As we enter the new century, there may be those who wonder what will become of the Church of the Nazarene. The purposes for which God called us into being—do those purposes still exist? As strongly as I know how to say this, I believe that they do. But if we are to follow the call of God on our lives and on our church, we must again commit ourselves fully to God in holiness, to one another in Christian community, and to the mission of the church in evangelism, compassion, and justice.

A JOYOUS GLIMPSE OF THE COMING KINGDOM OF OUR LORD

The following statement taken from the core values issued by the Board of General Superintendents describes our hope as Christians: "It is with a spirit of hope and optimism that we engage our God-given mission in the world. It is more than an expression of human concern or human effort. Our mission is a response to God's call. It is our participation with God in the Kingdom mission of reconciliation. It is the church's faithful witness to and expression of the love of God in the world—in evangelism, compassion, and justice. It is our faith in the ability of God's grace to transform the lives of people broken by sin and to restore them in His own image."

This is our hope as Christians. It is a hope based on faith in the transforming grace of God. It is our hope of the coming Kingdom.

While pastoring in Los Angeles, in urban San Diego, and now at Nazarene Theological Seminary, occasionally I would catch glimpses of the coming Kingdom. Imagine this—

- People from 30 nations standing together singing "Amazing Grace" in half a dozen different languages.
- People who were hard-core homeless drug addicts testifying by their words and changed lives to the transforming grace of God.
- A Communion scene with Christian brothers and sisters coming forward to receive the elements—rich and poor; Black, white, yellow, and brown; young and old; Sudanese, Cambodian, Latino, Haitian, and Anglo-Saxon; healthy, sick, and dying with AIDS—an extremely diverse group, but one in Jesus Christ.
- Food lines where the poor are greeted in the name of Jesus—and offered the dignity of stepping to the other side of the table to help serve.
- Health care, job training, and tutoring offered through the week to those in need.

These glimpses of the Kingdom are, for me, full of power and love and sheer joy. They are moments when I stand with a group of people in full anticipation of the final day when we will all be with Christ. For me, they are pictures of who we are at our best and who we are becoming as people of the Kingdom.

THE COST AND MEANING OF
BEING TRULY MISSIONAL

The call to be a Kingdom people does not come cheaply or easily. It comes with a price. We cannot be the people

God calls us to be without being a people of commitment. By the grace of God, we must be willing to respond freely and fully to the call of God. The call to commitment invariably moves us out of our comfort zones. Commitment is, by definition, not convenient. The commitments God calls us to, and that we must make, are counterintuitive and often countercultural. They are also true to the nature and spirit of the Kingdom.

As the people of God, we are called to be a holy people. When God makes us a holy people, He reproduces His own life in us. His very character takes form in us, so that as God is pure, His work of grace in us changes us into people of purity. As God is loving, merciful, and compassionate, His transforming grace changes us into people of love, mercy, and compassion. As the character of God is re-created in us, we find ourselves following Jesus into the middle of a broken world.

Our calling as the church is not necessarily to look for somewhere safe to hide, but rather to be the people of God in the world—to be fully *in* the world but not *of* the world. The call of God is for us to take up residence in our world—to be an incarnational presence of compassion and hope. It is who we are: the Church of the Nazarene, a church for all people.

It's in our bones!

—○—

We need to be able to see
what Jesus sees,
to hear what Jesus hears,
to touch what Jesus touches,
and to go where Jesus goes.

—Richard J. Mouw
in *Confident Witness—Changing World*
(ed. Craig Van Gelder)

—○—

CHOOSE LEGACY OR VENTURE CAPITAL?

Neil B. Wiseman

GOD'S GIFTS OF REDEMPTION from sin, human assets, and material blessings have made Nazarenes rich. Our magnanimous, spendthrift Father has blessed us "in the heavenly realms with every spiritual blessing in Christ" (Eph. 1:3).

Consider our magnificent assets. Every congregation has astounding human trophies of grace. Our cherished holiness-wholeness message answers the human quest for meaning by providing agape love, holy hearts, and enablement for service. And among our rich human resources are thousands who love the church enough to sacrifice or even die for her.

Eight liberal arts colleges, a Bible college, and a theological seminary provide the church an educated constituency. Modern publishing capabilities are owned by the denomination. Nazarene churches are located in every state of the union and in every province of the dominion. Global Nazarene missionary ministries are so extensive that the sun never sets on our worldwide missionary ministries in 135 world areas. The list of incredible assets goes on and on.

The future use of these treasures will determine what the Church of the Nazarene will become in 10 to 20 years if our Lord tarries.

The key decision at this point in our history is the choice between maintenance and mission. *Maintenance* means protecting or even hoarding what we have. *Mission* means using every imaginative effort and resource to take Jesus to the most spiritually needy person in your community and around the world.

Will It Be Legacy or Venture Capital for Christian Usefulness?

For several years I have written and preached about my concerns for the aging of the Church of the Nazarene as she nears her 100th birthday. Her age puts her at risk for heart failure. Other aging symptoms include subtle dangers like hardening of categories, safety in personnel choices, arguments concerning revivalism and evangelism, fear of church planting, and ambiguous preaching concerning a pure heart and a holy life. The aging process means decisions take longer, resistance to change is greater, and willingness to travel new roads keeps decreasing.

Meanwhile, the accumulated assets from 100 years of Nazarene history are sufficiently large to keep the church going for 50 more years. That could be tragic. Like spoiled rich kids who inherit money they never earned, our churches would likely become soft, weak, and irrelevant with a diluted message.

As the church approaches the century mark, her inheritance will soon pass to a new generation. The question is whether this new generation will choose to live off the legacy or to invest the inheritance as venture capital to multiply and fulfill its mission.

A Pioneer Agenda and Perspective for the New Century

I propose we work hard with every muscle and imagination to find ways to replicate and rekindle the all-out, do-or-die commitment of Bresee, Wesley, and Luther. Those pioneers knew the gospel, understood their times, and creatively connected the two for Christ. In shorthand spiritual language, it means setting our agenda according to God's priorities for our times.

God intends for us to tap into His strength, wisdom, and power to accomplish His agenda for our times.

God intends for us to tap into His strength, wisdom, and power to accomplish His agenda for our times. I am beginning to believe one great hindrance to the gospel's impact on our times is the energy good Christian people spend fretting over how bad things have become in our world. Regardless of how bad it gets, the church is still the missional people of God whom He wants to use to accomplish His purposes. And even in the worst of times, the church in partnership with her Lord can be invincible.

That means every church and pastor must seek to know God's missional agenda according to His priorities for His Church. Profound advice for setting such an agenda comes from author Henry Blackaby: "Our role as a church is to be his body that he will use to accomplish his work through our ministry to others. . . . Churches are to be constantly in mission with Christ redeeming a lost world" (*The Man God Uses,* 125).

To build a great future, the spirit of the pioneers must be recaptured so churches take the gospel with creativity and imagination and effectiveness into the crannies of contemporary culture, into the empty lives of millions who have tried nearly everything else, and into the open hearts of immigrants.

My vision for contemporary pioneers is forward, rather than backward, with a spirit that impacts our times like past spiritual influencers impacted theirs. It's a journey of the heart, caring for what is closest to the heart of God and serving those who mean so much to Him.

This Is Our Day for Missional Ministry

Never forget one sobering fact: This time is the only time we have to do ministry. Every generation has its own time to make a difference for God. These are the only days we have to do what the Creator had in mind when He made us.

But be encouraged. God was here long before we arrived. These times do not threaten or surprise Him. Since they are the only times we will ever have and since we believe the sovereign Lord placed us in this period of history, then He surely expects us to offer people a church that will attract them in seeking Christ. And He promised to be with us.

My obsession is that we learn all we can about how effective leaders of the past exegeted their period in human history and their setting for ministry. Certainly Luther's Germany, Wesley's England, and Bresee's Los Angeles were significantly different. But all three spiritual pioneers demonstrated by their ministry that they knew their times well. With that understanding in hand, they effectively applied the gospel to their world.

Have You Heard the Stirring and Considered the Possibilities?

In answer to the prayers of many persons who care about the Nazarene future, an amazing something is happening. Local, district, and denominational leaders have started a quiet spiritual revolution called *missional*—a word not found in many dictionaries. Beyond any attempts at definition, *missional* describes a contagious, creative new spirit starting to sweep across the church.

To be candid, few Christian groups have ever been able to retain significant spiritual vigor into their second century of existence. But in many places, Nazarenes are saying,

"Why not try?" If we can lick the common defeating trends, we can have *at least* another 50 years of Christ-exalting service. Surely the sovereign Savior is as willing to work through established churches as He is willing to create new organizations as needed for His redemptive purpose.

This call to become missional is not just a program or slick campaign, but an authentic call to more fully understand the essentials of the gospel.

Claude E. Payne and Hamilton Beazley describe a missional congregation and explain the healthful benefits that arise from missional commitment: "Such a community of believers embraces the power of prayer and recognizes divine involvement, encounters the holy in daily life, and is confident of experiencing miracles and God's ever-faithful care. In this kind of community, miracles occur and are recognized, lives are changed, and the joy of transformation is spread from disciple to disciple and from disciples to the spiritually hungry and unchurched" (*Reclaiming the Great Commission*, 52).

The new missional emphasis provides the exact focus and encouragement Nazarenes need for rediscovery of purpose, renewal of vision, and revival of passion. This call to become missional is not just a program or slick campaign, but an authentic call to more fully understand the essentials of the gospel, to more accurately exegete our environment so we know our circumstances, culture, and people better than anyone else—including the natives—and to apply the adventures of Christ to modern living.

The potentialities of becoming a missional movement provide us many new opportunities for increased effectiveness. So rather than allowing secularism to drown the church, we can seize secularism as a gigantic mission field that desperately needs the gospel. Living and working in this mission field means clergy and laity alike learn the language, understand the customs, and develop unique ministry methods just as missionaries do in fields outside North America.

Making the Future Spiritually Vigorous

I have changed my pessimism concerning the church's future. It can be bright and beautiful as she responds to the missional challenge. I believe the church in many places is experiencing new life because so many are praying and working to make local churches more missional.

After years of being anxious about our church's spiritual future, I feel inspired by the possibilities represented in being missional. My soul is full of thanks to God, my energy renewed, my imagination stretched, my hope resurrected.

Look at how God is fulfilling His promise before our eyes that in these last days "I [God] will pour out my Spirit on all people. Your sons and daughters will prophesy, your young men will see visions, your old men will dream dreams. Even on my servants, both men and women, I will pour out my Spirit in those days, and they will prophesy" (Acts 2:17-18).

Significance of Missional Service

No one fully comprehends the practical and eternal significance of pastors, churches, and districts becoming missional. But at the basic minimum, *missional* must mean we will share the gospel as creatively and vigorously next door, down the freeway, and in the next town or city as missionaries do around the world. This concept squares with Scripture and brings to pass Dr. Bresee's charge that we are to give the gospel to everyone in the same measure as we received it.

Could it be that God's directive for our future is found in a renewed practice of a biblical missional emphasis? I am tremendously encouraged by the possibilities.

What Does *Missional* Mean in Your Present Assignment?

Check out the teaching of Scripture. Nearly every page of the Gospels shows how Jesus lived out a missional passion for everyone He met. His teaching about *missional* is more demonstrative than conceptual. Fuller Theological Seminary President Richard J. Mouw in the book *Confident Witness—Changing World* gives one biblical example when he underscores the missional strategies by the apostle Paul:

As I look for biblical resources for missionary methodology, I am very impressed with the way in which the Apostle Paul made his case on Mars Hill. The basics of the story in Acts 17 are familiar. Paul meets a group of Greek philosophers, Stoics, and Epicureans, who invite him to present his perspective on reality. . . . He presents a profoundly biblical and practical missionary methodological model. First, he knew their writings and was conversant with their poetry. Second, he had discerned an underlining spiritual motif, observing that "I see that in every way you are very religious." Third, he looked for positive points of contact within their world view, noting what even their own poets had said. And finally, he invited them to find their fulfillment in the person and work of Jesus Christ. (7-8)

In a more contemporary time frame, my church planter friend Craig Winesett gave me his list of characteristics of a missional pastor. The headings are his and the explanations mine.

1. Study the culture. What about the culture where you live and minister is friendly to the gospel? How do the people think? What are their needs and interests that could be used to introduce them to Christ?

2. Question hindering conditions. What keeps you and your church from spiritual breakthrough? What conditions can you change? What hindrances are merely misinforma-

tion or self-imposed fears or hindrances? Who is ready to
receive the gospel this minute?

3. Get acquainted with new people. Talk to your neighbors. Ask the opinion of shakers and movers of your community. Discover the key to their hearts.

4. Learn the language. How do the people talk? What
do they mean? Find ways to sharpen your understandings of
what secular people mean when they are in conversation
with you.

5. Resist isolation. Our doctrine of separation often
takes us away from people. You can love people and even
accept them without approving everything they do. *Missional* takes us into the lives of people.

6. Try new methods. Congregational leaders sometimes
confuse message with method. The message is changeless;
the methods change in every generation.

7. Confront and expand your comfort zone. Most
church leaders cannot become missional until they are willing to identify and expand their comfort zone. Perhaps every
great work for God has sent persons to do some new thing
they have never done before.

8. Give attention to neglected populations. Here's a
short list to prime your thoughts: blended families, persons
of a higher economic class than yours, new retirees in small
towns and rural communities, migrant populations, second-
generation language groups, apartment dwellers, new profes-
sionals (doctors, lawyers, teachers), and disturbed children.

Missional Has an Amazing Impact on the Local Congregation

Becoming missional will help us see souls saved and
grow strong Christians, even as it builds strong churches. It
develops spiritual muscles as it motivates generosity. It will
require that ministerial preparation be retooled. It will turn
Nazarenes into a holy force for God in Canada and the United States. It will strengthen us so we can do more for mis-

sions outside our borders. It will enable us to create new ways to deliver the gospel. It will clarify our perspective so we keep the main thing the main thing.

The idea is not less for regions beyond. Rather, it is a call for the church at home to match the spiritual passion and breakthroughs in other parts of the world. It means every believer becoming a missionary where he or she is.

1. *Missional* **requires prevailing prayer.** Prayer walks, prayer commitments, prayer promises, prayer cells, prayer letters, intercession, fasting, and prayer retreats are taking place in hundreds of places. When prayer is routine and perfunctory, the results are routine and perfunctory. But watch the results when a congregation gets serious about praying.

2. *Missional* **demands a desperate dependence on God.** Recall missionary stories from overseas outposts and how God came through. That's happening now in many settings. And it can happen in your setting too.

3. *Missional* **means expecting God to provide leaders.** So often the church says, "We will start a new work as soon as God sends a leader." *Missional*, on the contrary, means taking seriously the admonition of Scripture to pray for laborers and expecting God to answer.

4. *Missional* **requires thinking outside the box.** Stated in more lofty words, it means thinking in new paradigms. Doing ministry the way we have always done it will likely produce the same results we have always had. New ways of thinking means local churches—large, middle-size, and small—planting new churches.

5. *Missional* **means believing that resources flow to mission.** Thus, a missional leader never says, "We don't have the resources," but believes, "If God is leading in this new area of ministry, at the right time He will provide the resources." And He does.

6. *Missional* **weds the best of the new and old.** Depending on their experiences, Christian workers tend to choose between what was or what is yet to come. So disagreement and sometimes outright conflict take place between the young and the old or veterans versus newcomers. *Missional* combines the best of the past and the present.

7. *Missional* **must have the spark of God.** Missional strategies include many phases of ministry, but none will work without understanding and experiencing what evangelist Charles Spurgeon believed and preached: "If you want to move a train, you don't need a new engine, or even ten engines—you need to light a fire and get the steam up in the engine you now have. It is not a new person or a new plan, but the life of God in them that the church needs."

Remember the goal—every community a mission field, every church a mission station, and every Christian worker a missionary.

Becoming missional will give a new direction and increased empowerment to the details of your ministry.

Let's get in on what God is doing!

The winds of God—as Jesus described to Nicodemus and as the Early Church experienced on the Day of Pentecost—may not always go where we think they will, but they always take us where God is going and where He wants us to go.

And that is precisely where we want to be.

5

IN THE FLOW OF GOD'S MOVEMENT:

Challenge from the Board of General Superintendents

THE CHURCH OF THE NAZARENE has entered the new millennium. The 20th century's litany of tragedy is well known. Two world wars were fought, dictatorships rose and fell, and the Holocaust fixed itself in our hearts as perhaps the century's most troubling atrocity. But in response to these sobering realities, we declare that God through Jesus Christ has established His kingdom among us.

Major population shifts have transformed nations from rural to urban societies. Today nearly half of the world's population live in cities. As the world changed in the 20th century, so did the influence of Christianity. Over 2 billion people, one in every three, now claim the Christian faith. The Christian world has changed dramatically with the development of indigenous, independent churches in Africa and Asia, the rise of 20th-century Pentecostalism, and the fruit of thousands of missionary enterprises. In 1900 an estimated 60 percent of the world's Christians lived in Europe, compared to 25 percent today. Twenty-eight thousand people a day are coming to Christ in Asia and 10,000 a day in Latin America. One hundred years ago there were an estimated 8.7 million Christians in Africa. Today there are over 350 million.

Nearly a century ago, the Church of the Nazarene emerged as a united people. The movement to unify widely scattered regional Holiness churches culminated in significant mergers in 1907 and 1908. By 1915, what were once seven distinct parent bodies had coalesced into a single international denomination. Following a brief "retrenchment" due to the Great Depression and the Second World War, there was an explosion of missionary activity. The church responded to the youth movement of the 1960s by creating Student Mission Corps and youth-oriented singing groups as well as by broadening music styles. The church took seriously internationalization as it coped with the growing demands of its growth and cultural diversity. A new engagement with the city as a place of ministry and the rebirth of Nazarene compassionate ministries began in the 1970s.

We are radically optimistic about impacting our 21st-century world with the Holiness message.

At the turn of the 21st century, the future of this denomination has never been brighter. Many believe that we were raised up not for the 20th century, but for the 21st century. We are positioned to make a major contribution to our postmodern world. This affirmation is grounded in our Wesleyan-Holiness heritage with its radical optimism of grace. We believe that human nature, and ultimately society, can be radically and permanently changed by the grace of God. We have an irrepressible confidence in this message of hope, which flows from the heart of our holy God.

P. F. Bresee was fond of saying, "The sun never sets in the morning." It is still morning in the Church of the

Nazarene, and the sun never sets on our denomination around the world. We are radically optimistic about impacting our 21st-century world with the Holiness message. With clarity of vision, total commitment, and firm faith, we view the coming century as our day of greatest opportunity for making Christlike disciples of all nations.

But we must be sure of who we are.

At the recent millennium celebration, in response to requests from many sectors of the church, the Board of General Superintendents attempted to capture the imagination and passion of our church and its leaders with a declaration of core values. It reads in part:

Every organization that endures over time is based on a deeply shared combination of purpose, belief, and values. So it is with the Church of the Nazarene. It was founded to transform the world by spreading scriptural holiness. It is both a Great Commission church and a Holiness church at the same time. Our mission is to make Christlike disciples of all nations. . . . As the Church of the Nazarene transitions into the new millennium, it is appropriate to identify those distinctives that we joyfully embrace and celebrate. Our most precious treasures—our mission, calling, beliefs, and highest values—we gladly offer as a gift to the generation to come. We pray that our core values will continue to serve as a guiding light for those who must make their way through the light and shadows of the decades that lie ahead.

1. We are a Christian people. As members of the Church Universal, we join with all true believers in proclaiming the Lordship of Jesus Christ and in embracing the historic Trinitarian creedal statements of Christian faith. We value our Wesleyan-Holiness heritage and believe it to be a way of understanding the faith that is true to Scripture, reason, tradition, and experience.

2. We are a Holiness people. God, who is holy, calls us to a life of holiness. We believe that the Holy Spirit

seeks to do in us a second work of grace, called by various terms including "entire sanctification" and "baptism with the Holy Spirit"—cleansing us from all sin; renewing us in the image of God; empowering us to love God with our whole heart, soul, mind, and strength, and our neighbors as ourselves; and producing in us the character of Christ. Holiness in the life of believers is most clearly understood as Christlikeness.

3. We are a missional people. We are a "sent people," responding to the call of Christ and empowered by the Holy Spirit to go into all the world, witnessing to the Lordship of Christ and participating with God in the building of the Church and the extension of His kingdom (2 Corinthians 6:1). Our mission *(a)* begins in worship, *(b)* ministers to the world in evangelism and compassion, *(c)* encourages believers toward Christian maturity through discipleship, and *(d)* prepares women and men for Christian service through Christian higher education.

At the turn of the 20th century, the Church of the Nazarene was born. Phineas F. Bresee and others were deeply convicted that God had raised them up for the express purpose of proclaiming to the church and world the gospel of Jesus Christ in the Wesleyan-Holiness tradition. There are unmistakable marks of providence on this denomination. From a fledgling movement, the Church of the Nazarene now exceeds 1.3 million in membership and is ministering in 135 world areas.

The Church at Work for God

Your Board of General Superintendents brings good news of God's presence and blessing on the people called Nazarenes. During 1999 each general superintendent cared for two world mission jurisdictions that shifted midyear. In addition, each one was also responsible for 14 United States and Canadian districts. As servants of the church, we see a significant cross section of the denomination each year.

Catch a glimpse of the enthusiasm and vision of your Board of General Superintendents as they comment on the state of the church on February 27, 2000:

John A. Knight—In some quarters of the world there is hostility toward Christianity, evidenced by widespread persecution of Christians. There are also unprecedented opportunities for declaring the message of scriptural holiness. Hunger for reality in spiritual matters abounds, creating new receptivity to the power of redemptive love. Christ is building His Church. The next decade will be the most fruitful years in the short 100-year history of the Church of the Nazarene. Let's stay out of the way.

William J. Prince—Samuel Young observed that "the church is always on its last leg." It is imperative that the church must continually evangelize, or it will pass away. The opportunity of the Church of the Nazarene in the new century calls for every Nazarene to be a witness for Jesus Christ and to preach and live the sanctified life.

James H. Diehl—With an increased response to planting new churches across the United States and Canada, exceptional growth in the majority of the world mission regions, an overwhelming response to the evangelistic tool called the *JESUS* film, a record high payment of 97.21 percent to the World Evangelism Fund, I find it exhilarating to be a part of the Church of the Nazarene at the dawn of a new millennium. God has been preparing us for nearly 100 years for just such a day as this!

Paul G. Cunningham—After witnessing the incredible expansion of our work in mainland China, I am encouraged to believe we are on the threshold of a miracle in evangelism. Additionally the *JESUS* film reflects the hunger worldwide for personal, spiritual transformation. We are positioned globally for a historic harvest.

Jim L. Bond—God be praised for the truly remarkable

things He is doing through our church in 135 world areas. We are addressing human need, effectively employing creative forms of ministry, and building Christ-centered communities of faith. We must now intentionally refocus on our distinctive mission to live like Jesus in our personal lives and in our churches and engage the Spirit's resources in endeavoring to make Christlike disciples of all the world's peoples.

Jerry D. Porter—In spite of the difficulty and complexity of fulfilling our Lord's commission in this new world we live in, I celebrate the visionary determination and brave commitment to do whatever it takes to reach lost people for Christ and the Kingdom.

By the grace of God, this past year the Board of General Superintendents was privileged to minister in 68 world areas and preside at 182 district assemblies. We rejoice in the ordination of 253 elders and 6 deacons.

In the Flow of God's Movement

As we enter the third millennium and prepare to celebrate the centennial of the Church of the Nazarene in 2008, we want to stay in the flow of God's movement around the world.

Who are we? We are a brave band of 1,342,000 valiant Christian sailors traveling in a flotilla of 12,375 vessels with their respective pastor-captains. Some of the ships are large and elegant, carrying thousands on board. Others are simple, one-cell vessels with a score of sailors. Over our 92-year history, a rich diversity has emerged among these sailors, who speak more than 150 languages and hail from 135 world areas.

Where are we headed? We are on the move because God is moving us toward the helpless, lost, and broken ones around us. Every day 100,000 persons perish eternally without Christ. That is our mission. Actually, it is God's mission. Jesus portrays an omnipotent God who is on a mission to find the lost sheep, the lost coin, and the lost son (Luke 15).

The cosmic God is on a search-and-rescue mission, and we must join Him by proclaiming the arrival of God's kingdom and inviting persons to come to faith in Jesus Christ. We must rescue as many as possible as quickly as possible by extending to them the lifeline of God's marvelous transforming grace.

The Church of God has always been on the move. The first word in our Lord's Great Commission is *go.* We are not free to embrace the status quo of staying where we are. We must join His movement again and again.

Perhaps our greatest danger is that we will be so busy serving ourselves that we will miss the movement of the winds of God. We must set the sails to catch the full impact of the Spirit's wind. God is moving by His Spirit, moving all over the world. We must discover His movement and scurry to join Him.

Change is implicit in any definition of "movement." God himself is moving and changing His Church. I once heard L. Guy Nees assert that the Church of the Nazarene in her brightest hour was conservative in message and liberal in method. We dare not change the essence, but we must keep in the flow of His movement as He gives us new tools and methods to reach the ever-changing world we serve.

Where is God moving today? Where are the winds of the Spirit taking us? What marks of providence guide us into this new era? What are the signs of the Kingdom that we see in our world and in the emerging Church of the Nazarene?

1. Prayer and praise movement. There is a new and powerful rediscovery of the centrality of prayer in the life of the believer and the church. The storms we will face in this new century are far greater than our human capacity to withstand. We must passionately embrace an unswerving prayer ministry at the heart of all we do. May it be the preamble of every ministry voyage, and may a concert of prayer serve as the constant backdrop for all our labors. God is moving. Let us join Him by becoming a praying church.

2. Youth movement. As we begin this new chapter of ministry in this new millennium, we need to ask God to give us special grace to be effective in our ministry to children and youth. One-third of the world is less than 15 years of age. That's 2 billion persons waiting to hear about Jesus. Think of the cities of Boston, Bombay, or Berlin; they are "new" cities—a majority of their populations weren't even born 40 years ago. We have a wonderful privilege today of evangelizing, discipling, empowering, training, and deploying the youth of our generation.

Jesus Christ would not have been a builder (my dad's generation) or even a boomer (my generation). Jesus died at age 33. He was generation X. If the Lord answers our prayer for revival, it will come through the children and youth of our church. So let's empower them and follow them as God helps the Church of the Nazarene to be effective with children and youth.

William Prince said on one occasion, "We must give the church away, or we will lose it." Join the Messiah, who calls us to trust and give the church to the next generation now. We desperately need the creative and courageous leadership of generation X and millennium generation Nazarenes. God is moving among these young people, and we must let them lead us across the millennial bridge. We must declare a cease-fire in the generational and worship wars. We are one church, and we want the youth to begin to lead and serve with us, to the glory of God.

3. Multicultural movement. David McKenna spoke to the Free Methodist World Fellowship last June and said, "If one word sounds the keynote for the 21st century, it is the word 'global.' We talk about living in a 'global village,' depending upon a 'global economy,' communicating over a 'global network,' and planning for a 'global strategy.' It is time to think about being members of a 'global church.'"

We celebrate the global work of the Church of the Nazarene. God has blessed us with His missionary passion.

Our challenge is that every Nazarene congregation would be an inclusive church where anyone and everyone is truly welcome. We are one at the foot of the Cross. We dare not exclude any person from our ministry or fellowship. At the same time, we dare not massacre a minority's cultural values on the altar of the majority in the name of superficial integration. The universal Christ is relevant and resonates in every culture.

We have embarked on a great adventure: to be a truly global church. We are committed to the internationalization process "with rights, privileges, and responsibilities without limitation or stigma because of culture, color, or geographic location" (*Journal,* 22nd General Assembly, 1989, 298). Together we must tear down any walls of distrust, superiority, or power politics in the church that might separate us. We will join God's powerful global activity, giving the church to all Nazarenes without distinction.

4. Compassion movement. The distance between the wealthy and the poor of our world is greater than ever before. Idealistic humanism has succumbed to selfish hedonism. Greed and avarice continue to govern and to guide the destiny of our planet. What is the biblical response? Concern for the poor. Jesus himself identified with the poor.

Scripture testifies that there is a special place in the heart of God for the poor. Our church was born passionately embracing its mission to reach the disenfranchised and marginalized peoples of our world. Compassionate ministry is not something that we do—it is the lifestyle of the Spirit-filled believer. We do not minister to the poor in a condescending way. Rather, we respect, love, and serve them a cup of cold water in the redeeming name of Jesus. We embrace them on behalf of the humble Carpenter, and we give them the church. It is time to tear down the economic and class distinctions that might segregate us. May we be a sacrificial, generous body of believers in honor preferring one another, to the glory of God.

5. Evangelism/discipleship/church planting movement.

There is a great moving of God's Spirit in the church today. It is a new zeal and determination to proclaim the gospel in a winsome and effective way to evangelize the lost. Whether we use evangelistic revival crusades, the *JESUS* film, "each one reach one," or friendship evangelism, we must scurry to keep in step with God's enthusiasm for reaching the lost. Nearly 900,000 new Nazarenes joined our global church family during the past decade. Last year alone, an average of 257 new Nazarenes joined our church family every day. Every 14 Nazarenes led one person to faith in Christ and membership in the church.

Proactive and purposeful discipleship groups characterized the Wesley Revival. These "classes" included weekly prayer, doctrine, and Bible study. Class members were invited to join a society, and they were further urged to join a "band" for "any Methodist serious about pursuing Christian perfection" (*The Upward Call*, 155). Sincere and even blunt accountability characterized these weekly spiritual growth meetings. The Great Commission is more than evangelism. It is also a call to "make disciples" (Matt. 28:19). By the grace of God, our worldwide church family has grown to a total of 1,342,252 persons who have been incorporated into the Body of Christ.

Church planting is a natural and necessary outgrowth of evangelism and discipleship. New communities of faith become centers of Bible proclamation, doctrinal teaching, fellowship among believers, and launching pads for outreach ministries to a lost and dying world. Today we have 12,375 churches worldwide and many more church-type missions. We must not rest until churches have been planted in every community around the world. In addition, these congregations must resonate with every culture of every person in every community.

The challenge we face is overwhelming. The world population did not reach 1 billion until 1804. It reached 2 billion 123 years later, in 1927. By 1960 there were 3 billion. Then the population exploded to the next billion in only 14 years, followed by another billion in 13 years; and after only 12 more years, in 1999, our planet's population surpassed the 6 billion mark.

We must move courageously to multiplication strategies that will allow us to reach this generation for the Kingdom.

Even as the Christian Church grows, there are more and more lost people every year. During the 20th century, that number jumped from 1.2 billion to a staggering 4 billion persons. Nearly 6,000 people will pass into eternity while we read this report; two-thirds of them will die without Christ. Our Lord would not have us embrace the status quo of our past. His commission is clear. We must move courageously to multiplication strategies that will allow us to reach this generation for the Kingdom.

Rick Warren reminds us that a "it is natural for [the Church] to grow if it is healthy. The Church is a body, not a business. It is an organism, not an organization. It is alive. If a church is not growing, it is dying. . . . The key issue for churches in the twenty-first century will be church health, not church growth. . . . When congregations are healthy, they grow the way God intends" (*Purpose Driven Church*, 16-17). With God's help, we will nurture and multiply healthy disciples, pastors, and churches in order to fulfill our Lord's mission.

So are we yet a movement, or are we simply an institution that once was a movement? In the truest sense, we never were the movement. It was always *God* who was the movement. We joined His mighty movings. We must do it again. We must purposefully and obediently move into the mainstream of His activity. As a church, we must become a *prayer-youth-multicultural-compassionate-evangelistic movement.* We are joining God's transforming *Holiness Movement.*

As we move toward the Nazarene centennial celebration, your Board of General Superintendents, in consultation with church leaders, would invite you to join us in a faith-vision of our church for the year 2008.

VISION 2008

• We pray for a harvest of 1 million new Nazarenes in eight years, embracing faith in Jesus Christ and joining our global church family.

• By God's grace we envision a global membership of 2 million Nazarenes and 2 million persons in weekly attendance by 2008.

• The passion of our Lord to go to all the towns and villages challenges us to launch new centers of holy fire allowing us to visualize 18,000 churches worldwide by 2008.

Is this challenge too small? Would the Lord want us to be more courageous and impassioned? This is the official centennial challenge from your Board of General Superintendents; but would the Lord want His Church to move from addition to multiplication?

If each Nazarene congregation would launch a new faith community every three or four years, we would celebrate our centennial with nearly 50,000 church fellowships. If each Nazarene would bring one person to Christ and the church every three or four years, we would report over 5 million Nazarenes by 2008.

As we move into this new millennium, God is already here, moving His Church by His Spirit. There are no spectators on these vessels. We must all join our Commander with a new oath of allegiance. We are a mighty movement, because God is moving us by His Spirit. We plead for the Father, in His mercy and grace, to deliver us from the soul-damning safety of the status quo. We yearn to catch the wind of His Spirit taking us and making us a mighty, transforming force in this generation.

Paul Cunningham quoted Robert Quinn in a recent editorial: "We 'walk naked into the land of uncertainty.' Isn't that what the call of God always requires? To give up our pretense and position, our safety nets and comfort zones, and walk naked into the land of uncertainty. . . . Frankly, my heart longs to be part of something that is so full of God, so overwhelmingly challenging, that we . . . stand before Him, trembling with fear—something heart-pounding that would shatter our calendars and test the realm of believability— something that would make us stammer and stutter . . . because the overwhelming immensity of the task is so far beyond our wildest imagination to accomplish. Wouldn't that be something."

The chairman of our board concludes, "May the days of the new millennium blaze anew with a fresh vision of all that yet could be through a revived church—an all-out-for-souls church" (*Holiness Today*, January 2000).

Respectfully submitted,
John A. Knight
William J. Prince
James H. Diehl
Paul G. Cunningham
Jerry D. Porter
Jim L. Bond

Prepared and presented by Jerry D. Porter for the Board of General Superintendents

—○—

Globalization is now leading to multiple
ethnic cultures and racial traditions living
together in the same neighborhoods.
With increased immigration and migration
to North America from all parts of the globe,
more persons now come into direct contact
with cultures, religions, traditions
other than their own.

—Craig Van Gelder
in *Missional Church: A Vision for the
Sending of the Church in North America*
(ed. Darrell L. Guder)

—○—

6

THE CHANGING FACE OF THE CHURCH

A Panel Discussion from the October 2000 Gateway to the World Conference

CHANGE AND CRISIS face every part of the Church, including the Church of the Nazarene. God has placed our denomination in this unique time to impact millions who desperately need the Lord. To do such highly significant work, urgency is required, and setting priorities according to God's agenda is absolutely necessary. To do that effectively, we have to have a thorough and accurate understanding of our times.

Population change is everywhere evident. Watch passengers in any major airport, and you realize the United States and Canada are countries composed of many nationalities, languages, and customs. In both countries, because many extended family members became citizens within the last 100 years, we have either family experience with being immigrants or personal experience with welcoming immigrants.

What is new is unfamiliar cultures, strange-sounding languages, and confusing religions. For example, in the not-too-distant past, most retail personnel looked like white American society, but an east Indian woman with a heavy accent, whose head was covered in observance of her Eastern religion, served shoppers during the Christmas season in a major Kansas City department store.

The foreign-born population now appears to be increasing in many smaller populated areas and inland cities.

A few months ago the Associated Press reported that more than 28.3 million—10.4 percent of the United States population—are foreign-born. The percentage of immigrants in the United States has increased from 4.7 percent in 1970 to 10.4 percent in 2000. Though immigrants have tended to settle in coastal states and large urban centers, the foreign-born population now appears to be increasing in many smaller populated areas and inland cities.

A few years ago, *Time* magazine published a special issue to describe the dramatic people changes taking place in the United States. Many changes resulted from a new wave of immigrant people coming from the Hispanic, Asian, African, and Caribbean areas of the world. These new citizens are literally affecting how we think about our country and how the church thinks about herself as she makes room for these new people in her congregations.

Our global effectiveness is well known. Our missionaries have been wonderfully effective in other world areas. Many immigrants entering our countries are Nazarenes, both leaders and laypeople, who found the Lord and became a part of the international church in their homelands. Now they bring excitement and commitment for evangelism and church planting to the North American church.

The panel members, who are experts in their field, are Dr. Roger Hahn, professor of New Testament, Nazarene Theological Seminary; Dr. Larry Lott, pastor of Blue Hills Community Church of the Nazarene, Kansas City; Dr. Jesse Middendorf, pastor of First Church of the Nazarene, Kansas City; Rev. José Pacheco, chairman of the Hispanic Strategy Committee for the United States; Rev. Mary Paul, pastor of

Bethel Church of the Nazarene, Quincy, Massachusetts; Dr. Stan Ingersol, archives manager at Nazarene Headquarters; and Dr. Tom Nees, director of Mission Strategy USA/Canada. We begin with Dr. Nees, moderator.

TOM NEES: Our purpose on this panel is to better understand the changing face of the Church of the Nazarene and changes in the culture of the United States and Canada. We want to discuss inevitable changes taking place in the Church of the Nazarene. But we also want to consider intentional changes that need to occur if we are to take full advantage of our new opportunities.

In thinking together about the changing face of the church, we already know most Nazarene congregations begin as a ministry to a specific location, so they are known, for instance, as the Church of the Nazarene at Blue Hills, or the Church of the Nazarene at Shawnee, Kansas. But for some hard-to-explain reason, most new churches quickly move from being a neighborhood-based congregation to a church serving most people who attend, regardless of where they live. Before long after their founding, most congregations tend to lose focus on their neighborhood. Then, to complicate matters more, the phenomenon of neighborhoods changing around the church is often viewed as a threat rather than an opportunity.

Why does a changing neighborhood make us so uneasy? Or perhaps we should ask, regardless of the change, how do we do better to make our communities our opportunities?

Dr. Middendorf, your congregation—Kansas City First Church—is making a concerted effort to be part of the neighborhood. How are you doing that?

JESSE MIDDENDORF: We do it through an intentional ministry called Neighbor to Neighbor. This plan targets a specific area around our church each year. We intentionally get into those homes three or four times a month with a significant contact through mailings.

NEES: What is your neighborhood?

MIDDENDORF: We have targeted a two-mile radius around the church, with about 8,000 homes, that we want to reach with the gospel of Christ and the message of holiness. Since we are mostly a metropolitan church with people driving in from many parts of the city, it is easy to give our full attention to those who attend. Having been in our present location for 16 years, we recognize the danger of becoming exclusively focused on the people who are already in the church. We want to stay in touch with the community, so we're intentionally trying to serve our neighbors.

Being community-focused is one way a church can address change when it begins to occur.

A problem Kansas City First Church faced in its previous location was that it did not stay in touch with its neighborhood during a time of extreme community change. Later the church tried to catch up, but it seemed impossible in the minds of decision makers.

Being community-focused is one way a church can address change when it begins to occur.

NEES: So the challenge is how to keep a congregation composed of commuting people connected to the church's community. How do the commuting people feel about emphasis on neighborhood ministry?

MIDDENDORF: Most buy into taking some degree of spiritual responsibility for our neighbors, though others are obviously threatened when all these new people show up.

NEES: What kind of "new people"?

MIDDENDORF: New means people our church members don't know. New people in our setting usually represents white, well-educated, middle-class families. In a commuting church, spiritually needy persons who live closest to our churches are often strangers. So we try to find ways to make contact with the community and provide methods for the community to respond to the church. We host a number of community activities and events and even serve as a polling place. I'm actively involved in community issues. We try to keep interaction very intentional, especially with spiritually needy people in our community.

NEES: You referred to Kansas City First's previous experiences in another neighborhood. It's interesting for our discussion that the area of Kansas City that First Church left is the neighborhood where Dr. Lott serves the Blue Hills Community Church of the Nazarene.

MIDDENDORF: That's true. Relationships between a long-established church moving from an area and a newer church developing in the same area create a facility dilemma for everyone. That's exactly the situation with Kansas City First Church and Kansas City Blue Hills Community Church. Though I was not pastor at KC First Church when the relocation took place, I am well aware of some of the difficulties.

A serious issue for missional focus for the relocating church and for the district is how we dispose of properties or how we transfer properties. Regrettably, in most situations, a growing congregation serving in the same neighborhood in inadequate facilities makes it almost impossible to take advantage of growth opportunities.

At the same time, it must be admitted that First Church needed the equity to relocate. Then, too, the worship space in the old property might not fit the worship preferences of Dr. Lott's church. All these issues are not always clear and certainly not easy to sort through.

In similar situations, what are we going to do in the future to be sure that as churches grow and as they move from place to place we don't disinvest in neighborhoods and abandon future Nazarene potential ministries to the areas being left?

LARRY LOTT: That's a good question, a practical question for our congregations. I think it would have been helpful if some kind of presence had been left in our community. I'm not sure of all of the reasons, but I imagine one reason for the move was that most members lived in other neighborhoods. It seems that the church relocated to be nearer its people.

But like Dr. Middendorf expressed an eagerness to impact their present neighborhood, something intentional was also needed to assure that a Holiness, Evangelical presence was retained in their community.

NEES: Practically, the church that relocates wants to sell their existing property to have financial resources they need to relocate. How can they maximize the resources and still maintain a presence?

The community they abandon is spiritually weakened.

LOTT: I understand the financial realities, but what about the spiritual needs of the community that often become more acute after a church moves away? The community I serve needed the spiritual strengths and ministries of First Church even though First Church felt it had to move.

NEES: What a dilemma. One church moves closer to where its members lives to be more accessible and to strengthen its impact on its member families. In the process, it seeks to win secular, upwardly mobile, spiritually empty people. They, in reality, move to a new mission field because they feel a spiritual obligation to their new neighbors. But the community they abandon is spiritually weakened.

Then the church that remains or the new church that is started usually does not have resources to finance or even maintain ownership of the facility the first church vacates and sells. So what needs to happen to do effective ministry in both settings? We will always have relocating churches. And we will always want to start new churches, even in old neighborhoods. How can these needs be balanced?

LOTT: Well, I think these issues are part of being in the Nazarene family. I think intentional decisions must be made whereby the property can be retained and yet a church like Dr. Middendorf's would still have enough finances from that building to actually use in their relocation project. At the time their congregation relocated, Blue Hills probably wouldn't have had enough money to purchase that facility, but we do now. Now we have a viable ministry in our community. Our church is a community-based body of believers with ministries to serve many different needs. Most of our congregation do not drive in from anywhere else.

One advantage of having the denominational family rather than being an independent church is that you have resources to help in that sense. Perhaps we need a property holding agency or some responsible group to bridge the financial gap between the leaving church and the emerging church.

NEES: When you consider it carefully, it's amazingly self-destructive to sell a building in areas where we'll eventually return. But that's what we do, and that's one of our greatest hindrances for starting new works in cities—finding affordable property for urban churches.

MIDDENDORF: Somewhere in these realities we have been discussing, it seems like a partnership is needed between local churches, districts, and the denomination so we don't leave behind a community without some means by which they would have a beginning resource to solve the facility issue.

I look at the struggle the emerging church goes through. And I know that we as a local congregation now grieve over what perhaps we could have done to make that property available or to leave some significant resource for property available to them. Forging some kind of partnership that speaks to this need for ministry is crucial for Nazarene ministry of the future.

MARY PAUL: It seems that when relocation is considered, a question or call must be made to our people to relocate back into the neighborhood at the same time.

MIDDENDORF: Great idea—so you think a commitment to start a new community ministry in the old setting should become a natural concern and maybe even be a required part of relocation.

More and more Nazarenes are starting to realize our effectiveness means we must welcome diversity.

PAUL: There may be a surprising and expansive missional issue here. There may be a dual demand by God's Spirit when relocation is being considered. So the first question is whether a church is really being called by God to move to a new neighborhood. And if the answer to that question is yes, then what is the congregation's responsibility for meeting the spiritual needs of the community they leave behind. So maybe a congregation that plans to relocate starts by beginning a new church one year before it plans to move. Or for churches that relocated years ago, maybe God wants them to go back to start a new church in the area they left. That might produce hundreds of new urban churches.

NEES: Let's face realty. Relocation is frequently driven by "changing neighborhoods," a euphemism used in the English-speaking white community for people not like us who are moving in. But history shows that moving away doesn't make a church spiritual or effective.

More and more Nazarenes are starting to realize our effectiveness means we must welcome diversity within our local congregations as well as in the denomination.

I would like to think of the goal as being an inclusive church.

ROGER HAHN: How do we develop cross-cultural skills and express loving acceptance? And how we do teach shy, fearful people to reach across these barriers?

NEES: It's tough, demanding work, but it has to be done. To understand and work effectively with diversity, we must develop cross-cultural skills that we thought were needed just for overseas missionaries. Now every minister and lay leader needs multicultural awareness and understanding. He or she must learn to accept everyone he or she meets and to see people with the eyes of Jesus.

MIDDENDORF: Let's think of what that really means. How does one become multicultural? What skills do we need to develop inclusive churches?

JOSÉ PACHECO: To being multicultural I would equate to being an international church. To me, it's not the specific ABC's of a rigid formula. Rather, it's a spirit of inclusiveness, of acceptance, of unity with diversity as we see in the Book of Acts. You have to capture the spirit of being multicultural.

Last year in a TEACH Conference I attended, a pastor asked, "Give me the ABC's of how to reach the Hispanics."

I replied, "It's difficult to put it in an ABC formula. But before anything else, you have to have the spirit of being international Christian."

NEES: Becoming an international Christian?

PACHECO: Exactly—become an international Christian. Then, I think, we must deal with issues of fear and respect.

To minister to persons of a different background, you have to overcome your fears of going to another culture. Fear is usually just a myth in your mind; nothing bad will happen just because you try to reach across social and language diversities. In fact, when Hispanics have moved into your community, they are interested and sometimes eager to be accepted by persons who are part of the United States and Canadian culture.

Respect for another person's background is the other issue. Another culture is not better or worse than yours—it's just different. And we have to stress that point all the time. If I want to respect another culture, I must view it as neither inferior nor superior to mine—but different. And if we can let that respect show to others, I think it will help us be international in our outlook.

And if I put a C to our A-B list of answers, I say go for it. Do something. Try it in your community. Most of the hindrances are long-developed myths that simply are not valid.

MIDDENDORF: He's discussing an issue at the heart of small-church culture. You're talking about overcoming fear. You're dealing with reasons why people attend this little church. All this feeling of comfort makes it difficult for anyone to reach across to another culture—even to people with the same language and culture.

NEES: The goal of a multicultural church is not to get everybody to look alike, but for a congregation to come to the place in which we celebrate cultural diversity as an advantage.

MARY PAUL: Fear, respect, and lack of experience are all part of this complicated effort to develop inclusive churches, aren't they?

NEES: You're right, and we all have to work at understanding and even correcting these difficulties. Racism must be called sin that requires forgiveness and repentance. Prejudice must be questioned and shown to be false. And persons who are members of the majority and the minority must be taught to accept, celebrate, and express agape love in spite of the differences in our backgrounds.

The power of Christ goes beyond the barriers of domination and discrimination.

Let's bring into our discussion an excerpt from a message by Dr. Paul Cunningham at the 1994 Multicultural Conference in Nashville. In this message he addresses the church's role and responsibility regarding diversity, prejudice, and racism. Let's hear him.

PAUL CUNNINGHAM (by video): The power of Christ goes beyond the barriers of domination and discrimination. His power goes beyond all of sin's barriers, and our mission is to get the word out, to not focus on the barriers, but to focus on the mission and get the word out. This is the word they need in Bosnia, where racial and religious discrimination are causing neighbors to slit each other's throats. And these are educated people. You remember Joseph Goebbels, one of Hitler's prime assistants, had a Ph.D. Education alone is not the answer. It is only the cross of Jesus Christ that is big enough and strong enough to destroy the monster of sin. And we must remember as we work together in celebrating our diversity that discrimination, prejudice, domination may be sin issues. It's a sin issue. Color it any way you want to, but it comes down to being a sin issue.

I believe cultural diversity is providing us with one of the greatest opportunities the church has ever had because we have the message that enables us to live together and enjoy each other at God's table. That is what our message does for us. You can't hate somebody and have holiness of heart and life. You can't be discriminating against somebody if you have holiness of heart and life. The two do not go together, you see. They just don't go together. That's why this message is a message that the world needs to hear."

NEES: Dr. Hahn, this is a theological issue as well as a practical issue. Dr. Cunningham addresses it very forthrightly. What do you make of this?

HAHN: Well, obviously I agree with my general superintendent, but it's been a theological issue all along; even our discussion shows that. We won't solve these issues with just some organizational fix. Rather, the solution first of all starts with a vision of what the church is. A part of what the church is for us is a holy people. What Dr. Cunningham said is certainly true to Scripture—hatred and racism and holiness of heart are incompatible.

I think for some believers it presents a difficult but necessary transition. So often we have thought of holiness only in terms of my relationship to whomever I know—a kind of individualistic issue between me and my family and friends. As a result, we have been unaware of the Holiness implications for institutions and systems and societies.

To change our perspective, or maybe I should say *assumptions*, we need a process to develop an awareness that even though holiness of heart instantaneously addresses my wholehearted commitment to Christ, there will arise now and again moments of awareness of new areas of need. It is what old preachers called light, where I am suddenly confronted through some other person, through a ministry of the church, through meeting an individual of another race, or through the witness of the Holy Spirit that my attitude toward a person or a group is sinful.

NEES: Can we articulate holiness in a way that deals with this issue of diversity, racism, prejudice, and perfect love directly?

HAHN: I think we are better equipped than any other theological system, but we do need to strengthen and embrace both entire sanctification as a crisis experience and the growth that follows.

For many, the crisis experience doesn't deal with racism. Often the seeker for holiness is not aware of racism. It is that unfolding, walking-in-the-light process that we may suddenly discover, "Ah—in light of what I am feeling, God is calling on me to have an understanding of the church and of people that's more than just social and more than just comfortable. It's directed of God, and I've now got to shift my beliefs and behaviors from the way I was raised or the way all my friends think about others to the way God thinks about them."

NEES: The charge, of course, has been that the church has caused a lot of prejudice, if not outright racism. Rather than supplying an answer, it's been a part of the problem. To the degree that it's true, how do we turn it around?

HAHN: I think to the degree it is true, we have to confess. My guess is that the degree to which it was true was the degree to which our view of the church is a social rather than a theological vision—that we wanted the church to be folks like us. We wanted it to be comfortable. And I want my church to be comfortable, too, but there needs to be this constant painting of the vision of "neither Jew nor Greek, slave nor free, male nor female" [Gal. 3:28]. That's part of the responsibility of every pastor, district and general leader, and theological educator to be painting this vision of what the church is and to keep inviting the people of God to that vision. It requires training key laypeople that this is what the church is. It is not about having a safe place to park our cars while we worship, but to be the people of God in the world, doing the work of God in the world.

LOTT: I think I agree with Dr. Hahn, but I'm struggling with one thing. And it's taken a long time from the standpoint of people who are oppressed to know how we should go about this. I think that perhaps in the face of slavery the church was silent, and when you put that up against the Wesleyan doctrine of the optimum of grace, I wonder how long it is going to take us to get to the place where God wants us to be.

HAHN: I don't know—I wish I knew. But I think we won't get there without confession. And it is a fascinating thing to me that the Southern Baptists only officially confessed to racism after over a hundred years of division over the issue.

NEES: These issues require leadership, and that means every one of us must use our influence to make it happen. How do we achieve the organizational changes needed to have a genuine multicultural church? We are underrepresented by minority people. Our minority church membership is between 10 percent and 15 percent compared to about 30 percent of the general population. Sometime in the mid-21st century, the English-speaking white population will become a minority. How do we get better representation in our leadership ranks?

Dr. Ingersol, you work with church history and trends. What do you want to say about these issues?

STAN INGERSOL: Two things I think could happen. One is that those who make appointments could appoint women and persons from minority groups so the makeup of different bodies and committees at district and general level accurately reflect the diversity within the church.

If you want a diverse makeup, you have to create the kind of committees and boards that you want now in order to reach that vision that you're pressing toward.

One need is a clear sense of the second chapter of Acts; the story of Pentecost has always been important in our tradition. We have always understood that our doctrine of holiness is related to the receiving of the Holy Spirit, but we have often exegeted and preached on Acts 2 in personal, individualistic terms. In that passage, we have different nations represented. In Peter's sermon, we have his statement that when the Holy Spirit is poured out, our sons and daughters will prophesy. And at the end of that chapter, we find a church that gives its goods in order to help the poor among its membership. It's a very radical chapter, but we tend to deal with only a narrow slice of it. In developing a more missional church, we need to come to grips with the whole theology that's embodied at Pentecost.

NEES: You've mentioned the issue of women in ministry. In the early days of our church, I've heard numbers that close to 30 percent of our ordained elders were women. My grandmother was an ordained elder, and she and my grandfather did pioneer ministry work; they say she was a better preacher than he was. When they went into neighborhoods to start churches, they worked together, and in my earliest days I remember women pastors and evangelists. But, Rev. Paul, we now have very few women in pastoral ministry. Why is that?

PAUL: I think several streams have affected our church's thinking and action on the subject. Some of that is a Fundamentalist theology that has closed doors for women.

NEES: How is that?

PAUL: Well, it's a clear denial of the Acts passage that speaks about sons and daughters. It basically insists that male leadership is God ordained and women are to do women's Bible studies or children's ministry—both valid ministries but not a box God created for us. And so that stream has affected the church.

Another issue is reaction to feminism. I think it's a reality that how you involve women in leadership is not only making broad decisions from the top but having pastors and laypeople at the grassroots level be a part of the calling forth of new leaders. I discovered in my own life that if I were to say I felt a call to full-time service at the college level and that I loved people, I was directed into social work. And I wonder if I came on that campus as a male and said those things, how different the reactions of faculty and administration would have been. Now God did not leave me there; He continued to give me a call that got more and more refined, and social work ended up to be a good base for me, but it's just interesting how we call forth people whom we are equipping.

One of the powerful things in my life was to find a senior pastor who believed in women in ministry. Out of his tenure at that church, four women were called and eventually ordained. It is because he sees them, he challenges them, he encourages them, he gives them places of service. I think there are women all over our denomination who are struggling with a sense of call but don't have anybody in a position of influence who says, "You know what that call might mean for you?"

NEES: But what happens to women when they have the call? Are there opportunities for them?

PAUL: That's when it gets difficult. The first church that gave me a call as solo pastor was an older church who remembered the days of the Church of the Nazarene when there were women evangelists, during the time when there were women pastors, and so it was interesting to me that it was an older church that called me. I began to hear about how churches who have people in the 30s, 40s, 50s were the ones that were completely closed to even looking at my résumé.

NEES: Are congregations ready, prepared for women as pastors?

HAHN: No, because they're governed by a social vision of the church rather than a biblical-theological vision of the church.

NEES: Meaning?

HAHN: Meaning that our group doesn't like women preachers. We don't think that's appropriate. That's not our comfort zone. Regardless of what Acts 2 says, this is the way we are. It's a social vision of the church.

MIDDENDORF: And we white, English-speaking males love democracy, because we can win. And we just perpetuate that.

NEES: When a congregation elects a pastor, it's more likely to be a white male than a minority or a woman.

MIDDENDORF: The church boards tend to function with that kind of priority in mind.

INGERSOL: What we need is a clearer sense of vision of the doctrine of the church on a church board. We should be involving people with different types of life experiences and people from different racial and ethnic groups, as well as women, so they bring their different life experiences to the dialogue, debate, and decisions. They help us make better decisions when we have such diversity there.

NEES: How has your congregation responded to you, Mary?

PAUL: Well, I've served two congregations now, and both have been incredibly positive and affirming, and I affirmed them back. They have given me a gift in giving me a place to serve; I know enough other women's stories to know that they have not had the same opportunities. I did not go to Nazarene Theological Seminary, but I hear from the president of NTS and others that women who graduate are left without a place to serve and end up going to other denominations. So I make sure I thank my congregation for giving me that call.

NEES: Well, it is time to bring this discussion to a conclusion. And if you would like a free video copy of *The Changing Face of the Church,* please contact the Mission Strategy office at Nazarene Headquarters, 6401 The Paseo, Kansas City, MO 64131—1-800-736-7167.

---○---

Change does not have to be bad
nor destructive.
Along with change come
new and exciting opportunities.
These can be put to work to catalyze
and motivate a ministry
to new accomplishments for the Savior.

—Aubrey Malphurs
Developing a Vision for Ministry in the 21st Century

---○---

7

BUILDING A MISSIONAL INCLUSIVE CHURCH

Jerry D. Porter

HEAR WHAT GOD SAYS about missional inclusiveness in His Church:

> The Messiah has made things up between us so that we're now together on this, both non-Jewish outsiders and Jewish insiders. He tore down the wall we used to keep each other at a distance. He repealed the law code that had become so clogged with fine print and footnotes that it hindered more than it helped. Then he started over. Instead of continuing with two groups of people separated by centuries of animosity and suspicion, he created a new kind of human being, a fresh start for everybody.
>
> Christ brought us together through his death on the Cross. The Cross got us to embrace, and that was the end of the hostility. Christ came and preached peace to you outsiders and peace to us insiders. He treated us as equals, and so made us equals. Through him we both share the same Spirit and have equal access to the Father. (Eph. 2:14-18, TM)

What a passage of Scripture to inspire us to build an inclusive church where every person is welcomed, valued, and needed! The apostle Paul challenges the Church in his time and the Church in our time with spectacular news:

Christ tore down the wall.
He repealed the law of fine print and footnotes.
It's a fresh start for everybody.
The Cross brought us together.
The Cross caused us to embrace.
Christ treated us as equals and so He made us equals.
Christ came and preached peace to both outsiders and
  insiders.
We both share the same Spirit and have access to the
  same Father.

After carefully considering Paul's anointed words, we grieve over any differences we have allowed to splinter His Body. In Christ we are one—none with privileged standing—all special and cherished by God. Christ brings us together, and at the foot of the Cross we embrace each other as equals.

On July 15, 1998, many of us gathered for the Multicultural Conference at Southern Nazarene University. I went to Oklahoma City with my comfortable Acts 2 sermon ready to be preached. However, after hearing several Black Nazarene ministers speak of the pain and frustrations they experienced serving as minority leaders in our fellowship, I felt compelled to ask them to forgive the white race and to forgive their church for these offenses. On my knees I asked Native American Johnny Nells to please forgive my race for all the broken promises and treaties, for the Trail of Tears, and for the present insensitivity to the plight of the nations he represents. I bowed at Roger Bowman's feet asking him to forgive me on behalf of my ancestors who participated in the African slave trade in order to create an economic system that would benefit the white race while denying that the African-Americans even had souls. I wept as I asked Roland Edouard from Haiti to forgive my generation for its prejudice that treats recent immigrants with disdain even as these workers are being exploited to provide inexpensive and abundant food for our tables. I asked these Nazarene church leaders to forgive our church for our insensitivity that forced them to "act, talk, and even think *white* in order to survive and minister in the ranks of the Church of the Nazarene."

Let's try a simple reality check. In which category do you fit?

1. You immigrated to North America during your lifetime; you were not born in the United States or Canada.

2. You are the child or grandchild of immigrants to North America.

3. You are the descendant of someone who immigrated to North America within the last 300 years.

Probably the only North American readers who have not yet found their category are the Native American brothers and sisters who have so graciously taken their time to read this book.

You see, an inclusive multicultural church is simply one that clearly communicates the message "Everyone is welcome here."

Let's consider three practical applications for contemporary Nazarene congregations as we gear up to increase our missional commitments in the United States and Canada.

1. How Willing Are We to Welcome Outsiders to Our Church?

Just how inclusive is your congregation? How ready and willing is your church to welcome people who are different from you? Consider six levels of inclusivity.

The Level One (least inclusive) church has ushers we might call church bouncers. Oh, yes—they are sincere, efficient ushers who dutifully collect the offering and help folks find a place to sit, but when *you* come to their church, if you're not like the rest of *them,* they gently guide you down the hall and downstairs to *your place.* Or perhaps they even say, "You know, you would feel a lot more comfortable if you would go down the street four blocks and two blocks to your left. The church there is just like you, and you would really want to be there, wouldn't you?"

Some feel that is racist, so at Level Two they train the
ushers to say, "Nice to have you here today. Please have a
seat" while thinking, "You really don't *belong,* and if we're
careful not to act too friendly, we would be relieved if you
chose not to come back. In the meantime, at least we can
count you, report a greater attendance, and we're glad to
take any offerings you choose to give to God's work."

Let's move up the spectrum a bit more to Level Three.
"Well, you've been coming to our church now for several
weeks, and it's almost district assembly time. Would you like
to join our church?" Now that's a major step. "It's one thing
for you to sit in our pews," they think, "but now we want
you to join our church. And would you tithe? We want you
to be part of us." Unfortunately, even after you join, you still
feel like an outsider. One man said, "I've been a member for
10 years, but I still don't belong."

Now for the fourth level of inclusivity. They don't have a
bouncer. They don't ask you to just *sit* there. They actually
let you join *their* church. Level Four inclusivity would help
you discover and develop your spiritual gifts and appoint
you to a ministry assignment. At this level you become a
part of the ministry team, and your name is placed on the
nominating ballot for church leadership positions.

Does the church want to be even more inclusive? Try
Level Five: "We would like to hire you to serve on the
church staff." When York, Pennsylvania, Stillmeadow
Church of the Nazarene hired African-American James Heyward as youth pastor, a new message went out to the congregation and community. As Rev. Heyward led the services
and preached, African-American worshipers commented to
Pastor Bud Reedy, "When I visited your church and saw
Pastor James on the platform as a staff member, I knew
there was a place for me here."

There is perhaps a sixth level of inclusivity—when a pre-
dominantly white church calls an African-American or a
Latino shepherd as their pastor. God's grace has broken

through a barrier. The apostle Paul said, "He [Jesus] tore down the wall we used to keep each other at a distance" (Eph. 2:14, TM). At Level Six, we are one by God's grace. And the walls have come down. That means that we are becoming as color-blind as God himself.

We all have racial and cultural roots. Most of us received Christ when He came to us wrapped in the swaddling clothes of our culture. There will always be some churches that focus on a particular target population, but at the same time *every Church of the Nazarene must always be inclusive. Everybody is welcome here.* We begin to understand the kind of church God wants to raise up in the 21st century: *a multicultural, inclusive, missional community of faith.*

2. How Willing Are We to Send Leaders to the New Mission?

So where are the missionaries we need to reach the people in this United States and Canada mission field? Where will these missionaries come from? Let's visit the congregation in Antioch as recorded in Acts 13.

Antioch First Church had a spectacular staff of outstanding leaders. Their congregation was blessed with a capable group of prophets, preachers, and teachers. There was Saul, Barnabas, Simeon, Lucius the Cyrenian, and Manaen, an adviser to the ruler Herod. That was a great pastoral team. They were doing a great work for Jesus their Messiah. They were having a wonderful time ministering, evangelizing, and discipling people in Antioch.

However, one day when they were praying and fasting, doing what they were supposed to be doing, God spoke to them: "I'd like these two leaders to leave this church."

"I beg Your pardon," they answered. "We have a huge 'Everybody Is Welcome Here' sign out front. We don't want any of our people to leave."

Yet God spoke: "Separate Saul and Barnabas."

They responded, "We couldn't make it without them.

What kind of a church would we have if You take Barnabas and Saul?"

We all shout, "Praise the Lord!" when Bill Sullivan challenges us, "Let's plant churches." But we hold our breath when Pastor Bob Huffaker from Grove City, Ohio, tells his church planting associate, "Recruit anybody you can from this church to go with you to assist you as you launch a new 'center of holy fire.'"

You see, to be the missional church that God wants us to become, we must be inclusive: "Everybody Is Welcome Here." At the same time, however, we must *release and send* key missional people to multiply the ministry. God may call some key people, some significant tithers, some talented workers to go to a new church, to a new mission field. In this inclusive missional church, we both welcome and send. It's all about God's kingdom. It's all His call.

3. How Willing Are We to Embrace God's Vision?

Move over to Acts 15. Paul and Barnabas finished their first missionary trip. They've had an awesome, fruitful tour. And, of course, their reports were fascinating. Their modus operandi was go to the Jewish synagogue in every community on the Sabbath to worship with the Jews. Then they would seek permission to use the synagogue on Sunday and use it for a time of Bible study. When Paul informed the decision makers that he had graduated from Gamaliel Seminary, they were usually sufficiently impressed to allow Paul to use the empty synagogue on the first workday of the week.

Paul shared the message of Jesus Christ as the promised Messiah and gathered the new Jewish believers as an embryonic congregation. He then took a quantum leap by preaching the glorious mystery that the gospel was for all people, all nations, all races, all colors, and all languages. Gentiles were invited to embrace faith in Jesus, the Messiah of the entire human race. Paul and Barnabas did that from town to town. Every indication is that Paul and Barnabas brought the Jews and Gentiles together into one congregation though they often met in homes as small cell groups.

Now they were getting ready for the second tour. Barnabas suggested, "Let's take John Mark."

"No, I don't want John Mark," Paul responded. "He's an irresponsible, immature missionary. He flaked on us in Thyatira. We're not going to take him again."

Nice guy, sanctified Barnabas proved to be just as stubborn as Paul. Finally Paul said, "We're not taking John Mark."

And Barnabas responded, "Then I'm not going with you."

Sometimes God uses a bit of sanctified discord to help us realize we could probably do better if we would just get a little distance and multiply our efforts. The missional church both welcomes and sends.

We might want our churches to live in such heavenly unity that we always hug and sing "We Are One in the Bond of Love." But our strategies and our passions sometimes differ. God may well allow these differences, dislikes, and preferences in order to multiply our effectiveness.

Do we really believe Paul and Barnabas were not following the Spirit when they refused to give in to each other? They were both a bit stubborn, and God encouraged or at least used their differences to launch two missionary teams.

Sometimes we're so cozy in our togetherness that we never go out to launch a new church. We can be so inclusive that we never *send*. An honest difference in focus or emphasis might help us say, "I love you, but I feel called to go and start a new church."

Out of the disagreement, Barnabas took John Mark and rescued him. Later Paul asked for him to serve on his missionary team, and Mark wrote the Gospel bearing his name. At the same time, Paul branched out with new staff members Silas, who was Jewish, and Timothy, who was Greek. This first multicultural missionary team accompanied Paul on his second missionary journey.

In Acts 16 the team went to Phrygia and then through the region of Galatia. The plan was to turn west and go into Asia. But the Holy Spirit blocked that plan. We don't know for sure what happened. Maybe Paul felt the Lord said no to him in his prayers, or perhaps the visas did not come through. Something happened, and Paul suddenly announced, "We're not going to go to Asia."

Paul was probably a bit embarrassed. Then he announced, "I don't know why God doesn't want us to go to Asia now, but we're going to go to Bithynia, straight north." By now the missionary leader had regained his composure and was ready to take his missionary troop to Bithynia. Then we read this fascinating comment: "The Spirit of Jesus wouldn't let them go there" (Acts 16:7, TM).

When Paul confronted two closed doors, he very wisely decided to take a little rest on the Mediterranean. He sat in a hammock under a palm tree and enjoyed the scenery. "Well, Lord, whenever You decide where You want me to go, I'll be here." That night Paul had a vision.

Paul had a vision. Please wait on the Lord. He wants to give you a vision. Some say it doesn't really matter what we do. They insist that God blesses whatever we choose to do. Well, I believe God is tolerant and patient with my preferences, but I prefer to believe that I can know that where I am going is where God really wants me to go.

You know why?

Pain and problems may be on the way. A few days after launching this ministry, Paul was beaten and thrown into prison. He sang praises to God while blood dripped down his back.

If I must shed blood, I want to know that I'm shedding blood in the right town. I really would like *to know that I know that I know that I know* that it was God and not my whim that led me.

Paul was energized by a vision from God. Pray that God will give you a specific, personal vision of what He wants you to do.

Paul had a vision of a man. A lot of us get excited about blueprints, but Paul saw a man. He didn't have a vision of a strategy or a slogan. He didn't have a vision of a building or a flowchart. He didn't have a vision of a program or a compassionate ministry center.

He had a vision of a *person.* That's what the gospel mission is all about. It's about reaching *persons.*

We sing that happy song, "Jesus loves me! this I know." We don't sing, "Jesus loves my soul and doesn't care about the rest of me." We simply testify, "Jesus loves me! this I know," which means He loves *all* of me. He cares about me emotionally, physically, socially, financially, and spiritually. God loves me. God loves people.

The vision God wants to give us is not primarily a ministry or program. By His grace, He will wrap His heart around your heart and send you to a person.

Paul had a vision of a man from Macedonia. When I was regional director in the Mexico and Central America (MAC) Region, I thought that it would be good to have pronounced the location of Paul's vision as MAC-e-donia. I needed more work teams who would respond to the plea, "Come over and help us!"

The Macedonian was the first European—white man—to be directly evangelized by this multicultural missionary team. That's when white folks were *outsiders* and the Jewish Christians were *insiders.* God said, "I don't want you to go to Asia right now; I don't want you to go to Bithynia. I want you to go to the Europeans."

When God gives you a vision, He will help you develop missional gifts so that you can identify and resonate with the culture of the persons to whom He sends you.

If God is sending you to work with Latinos, He has to help you learn to eat green peppers, beans, and tortillas. If God sends you to work with Koreans, you had better learn to love kimchi and eat with chopsticks.

God is not sending us to win a generic person but a man of Macedonia. We have to exegete the culture to which God sends us. Who is this person to whom God is sending me? What are his or her needs, lifestyles, and concerns? We will need to learn his or her heart language. Some people say about people of other cultures, "If they're going to come to America, they need to learn English" It's a very nice language for commerce and business. But when the Macedonian man is in soul anguish, he will pray and worship in his mother tongue.

The gospel of Jesus Christ, the Jew, came to us wrapped in the swaddling clothes of our culture. White North Americans see Jesus wearing blue jeans, driving a Chevy pickup, eating apple pie, talking English, and loving football. Cuban Christians view Jesus as a Spanish-speaking Caribbean Messiah who lives in the tropics, eats fresh coconuts and bananas, and plays soccer.

We have a great mission field in the United States and Canada. Among all the people groups in these lands, other than children and students, probably the most receptive populations are the recent immigrants. Would we be willing for God to give us a vision to reach these Macedonians and in the process be enriched by them?

Paul had a vision of a man from Macedonia who was standing. Sometimes we minister in a condescending way to the poor, the immigrants, the unemployed, the illiterate, and the handicapped. We, the "superior" ones, serve the "inferior" ones. But the man of Macedonia is not on his knees, he's not groveling, and he's not less than me. He is my equal.

There are no preferred races, classes, genders, or categories at the foot of the Cross. The ground is level—we're all the same there.

So could we respect and honor the people who share our church building? Could we treat them with love and dignity as our equals before God?

I don't know to which man of Macedonia God will call you. I don't know your neighborhood. I don't know what mission field you face. But I pray you will wait until you have the vision from God and that you will see a man of

Macedonia standing across the street, down the freeway, or in the next town who is waiting for you.

Paul had a vision of a man from Macedonia who was standing asking for help. The Macedonian man is not inferior to us. He is our brother on this planet, but he is asking us to help him. How can we help him? Paul immediately packed his bags and went to give the Macedonian man what he needed most. The European needed the invasion of God's transforming grace. The good news today is that you and I can make a world of difference in the life of the man from Macedonia. Our willingness to share the gospel story will revolutionize the temporal and eternal history of that solitary man in the vision.

Thank You, Father, for courageous Christians who have been baptized in holy fire that cleanses away racism and prejudice. Thank You for filling our hearts with Your perfect love, making us color blind so our hearts and our churches are truly inclusive representations of Your kingdom on earth. As we open our arms to include all as our brothers and sisters, we also commission, release, and send those You call to launch new ministries.

Lord, may we be the new missionaries You are calling. Grant us a perceptive vision of persons who belong to a particular specific culture and time. Infuse us with a vision for culture-specific persons whom we love and respect. Lord, grant us a culturally sensitive, passionate vision for persons who are our equals and yet who are very needy of the invasion of Your kingdom in their lives and communities. Let us be inclusive, missional, Kingdom communities of faith. Help us be as obedient to our vision as Paul was to his. In Jesus' name we pray. Amen.

Our church is a missionary church
that knows no difference
between home and foreign fields—
in these days all fields are near.

—Phineas F. Bresee
in *The Quotable Bresee*
(comp. Harold Ivan Smith)

PREPARING MEN AND WOMEN OF GOD FOR MISSIONAL MINISTRY

Neil B. Wiseman

MISGIVINGS ABOUT predicting the future increase when I remember the philosopher Uncle Josh's comment, "There is a great deal of speculation that is trying to untwist the untwistable. This is just about as smart as sitting down in a washtub, taking hold of the handles, and trying to lift the unliftable."

In spite of these risks of predicting the future, the significant responsibility for developing ministers for our new frontiers must be considered by all who have interest in the church's renewed missional commitments. Our task is to ask and answer the question, "What kind of ministers are needed for the new century?"

Two assumptions are foundational for developing missional clergy leaders—preparation ultimately belongs to the whole church, and to become a genuine missional leader one must think and behave like a missionary.

At the outset of this discussion, let's recognize the continual interplay in the preparation process between five factors: (1) the pastor's personhood, (2) the church's environment in the world, (3) the world, which includes society and culture, (4) the changeless gospel, and (5) the professor's attitude toward learning and the church. All these factors influence each other, but each also has a life of its own. And effective missional ministry in the United States and Canada must understand, shape, and use those factors in every preparation setting.

MISSIONAL ENVIRONMENT

The environment where ministry has to be done is experiencing the greatest upheaval to ever engulf the human race, and there is no reason to think it will slow or stop.

Just a few years ago, who envisioned a computerized society, fax machines, demilitarized USSR boundaries, redistributed global power, cell phones everywhere, or national leaders who compromise themselves by vacillation or outright defilement? These staggering changes make us believe new environments for ministry will be more secular, complex, and different from anything the church has experienced in 2,000 years—certainly unlike anything we have known in our lifetimes. Still, this is the environment in which God has placed us to do our work.

MISSIONAL CHURCH

The Church of the Nazarene, a part of the Church universal, is experiencing her own revolution—mostly a God-inspired revolution of missional approach to her work for God. Our church is significantly different than it was 10 years ago, but so is everything else. Efforts to refine our theology spawned unexpected side effects that gave us an identity crisis. That crisis has been greatly helped with the core values clarification by the Board of General Superintendents.

Ownership and content of clergy preparation are being reinvented and renegotiated, so every college religion department, district board of ministerial studies, and many pastors have assumed the role of judge to determine what a prepared Nazarene minister should be.

Rapid changes caused by a thousand colliding forces are reshaping Sunday School curriculum, revivals, book publishing, missionary giving, access to Nazarene higher education, pastoral relations, and representation to general assemblies. The list lengthens at a transitional time when denominational loyalty seems down and diversity up. To complicate matters even more, our congregations in too many places have settled for maintenance rather than committing to becoming a missional force in their communities.

In spite of these massive changes, think of our assets. The list is impressive. And the old preacher was right when he thundered from his pulpit the paraphrased words of Christ, "To whom much is given, much will be required" (see Luke 12:48).

Look at what we have and what we have already weathered.

A few years ago, no one would have believed that Nazarene pastors would be ministering to AIDS patients, single parents, drug addicts, blended families, sexually abused adults, homeless people, snooty boomers, new immigrants, or grouchy traditionalists.

Who thought pastors would be writing sermons on computers?

Who predicted increasing health insurance premiums might force us to close churches?

Who foresaw ministering in a world bewildered by medical ethics, baffling technologies, erotic details in the media, pornographic titillation on the Internet, and greed in every economic class?

These differences have us perplexed and dizzy, but it helps to hear Paul Harvey's words, "In times like these, it helps to recall that there have always been times like these."

Our present challenge—perhaps it should really be called a window of opportunity—is to find out how to use change as a superb opportunity to challenge ecclesiastical atrophy, to uproot unproductive methodology, to refocus our mission, and to deliver the gospel to the masses. I find management specialist Waterman's idea stimulating when he suggests change can "transform threats into issues, issues into causes, causes into quests." That's the grand potential of focusing ministerial preparation on missional ministry.

For our denomination, this can be our finest hour. Or it can be our frustrating aging cycle with hardening of the arteries, blurring vision, and deliberate deafness. The choice is ours. To design a compelling future on the creative edge of effective ministry will require a lot from all of us—like hearts on fire for God, aggressive imagination, deliberate risks, bravery to change methods, and fresh ways of thinking.

MISSIONAL CHALLENGE

As I read the situation, I see the most pressing challenge for clergy preparation is to help pastors in training learn to make our holiness/wholeness message understandable to contemporary people. Hungry unbelievers will be attracted when they realize our message offers wholeness, an attractive alternative to fragmented living. Our members will enjoy more rapid personal spiritual growth, too, when they grasp the possibilities of a holy life centered in Christ. And disillusioned believers from diverse religious backgrounds would join our ranks if they knew what we believe and teach.

To have a missional impact of massive dimensions like the Great Commission requires we must fully understand our strengths and commit to accomplishing our mission in light of contemporary realities. The possible victories are well worth every effort.

In this process of focusing on a missional future, too much attention to tradition will produce bewitching obsolescence, but it is obsolescence still. Wesley and Bresee were productive in their time precisely because they passionately proclaimed the biblical message in ways their contemporaries understood. Following their lead, we must train missional ministers to competently take the old message to the new generation.

I propose that an up-to-date understanding of our mission and purpose is needed without idolatry to history and without allowing fascination to fads. An uncomplicated, clearly stated vision could bind us together into an invincible force for righteousness.

I urge bold action. I propose exhilarating dialogue. I recommend we clearly identify contemporary battle lines. I suggest emerging issues be faced rather than wasting energies on outworn controversies.

I believe the Spirit of God may be pushing us to imaginative new clergy preparation to keep step with Him, so our motto is this promise from Scripture, "See, I am doing a new thing! Now it springs up; *do you not perceive it?*" (Isa. 43:19, emphasis added). I press for clergy preparation saturated with authentic spirituality, vigorous academic standards, vibrant imagination, and hard work.

Passionate Sense of Missional Potential

On pessimistic days I fear Southern Baptist evangelist Vance Havner's warning that religious organizations always run a ruinous course that moves from a man to a movement to a machine to a monument. It is sobering to ask where the Church of the Nazarene is on God's timetable.

On hopeful days, I believe intentionality, daring, and God-inspired strategies will enable us to become more missional in ministry. Kierkegaard expresses my excitement for our future: "If I were to wish for anything, I should not wish for wealth and power but for the passionate sense of the potential, for the eye which, ever young and ardent, sees the possible."

Now let us turn to specific proposals for developing stouthearted men and women of God for missional ministry.

1. The Mind of Christ

As a bedrock foundation for ministry, men and women of God must pursue the mind of Christ. He is the magnet that draws us all to Christianity. With its simplicity and depth, the mind of Christ is where vital piety and sound scholarship meet. Think of the appeal. A world, only slightly interested in spirituality, will be drawn to pastors whose ministries are filled to the brim with the resurrected life of Christ.

Beyond all theory-vs.-practice debate stands the absolute necessity that our churches must be led by Christ-centered thinkers who are loyal saints and ardent students of the Bible and life. Our graduates need to be trained to think like Christ. The raw materials for such thinking are His outlook, His values, His reconciliation, and His hope.

Let the mind of Christ be the frame of reference of our preparation, so students take their orientation, direction, and devotion from Him. Scholarship and spirituality in our church must always be judged by the mind of Christ.

2. Missional Achievement

Men and women of God for the new century must be passionate about achievement for the Kingdom. Let us agree—ministry means breathlessly trying to keep up with what Jesus wants done.

Regardless of how one defines effectiveness, more is needed. A burden for the world must infect our graduates so they live out the reality that ministry begins with a passion for evangelization next door, down the block, in the next community, in the nearest town, and everywhere else.

We do graduates an incredible disservice with preaching and teaching that praises faithfulness without results. Is it possible to be truly faithful without some apparent result?

The parable of the talents in Matt. 25 must be read again to hear Jesus reprimand the "no increase" steward as an "unprofitable servant" who is to be cast into outer darkness

(v. 30). Faithfulness in the parable is praised only in those who multiplied what was entrusted to them. Think of the implications of that idea for ministry in our time.

To become effective, graduates need to apply the gospel to human hungers in cross-cultural settings. They must learn to do the "critical few" things that generate quality and quantity growth.

3. Purity

Men and women of God for this massive missional ministry must be living examples of holy character made possible by the enabling Spirit of God. Pastors in the making need a personal Pentecost to cleanse their nature and to settle self-sovereignty. Lifelong intimacy with Christ is required if they are to effectively resist the temptations public life brings.

Close contact with Christ must lovingly force them to question their own playacting, duplicity, doublespeak, political upmanship, image building, and petty dishonesties. Pure talk authenticated by a pure walk is needed in every ministry assignment. Integrity, morality, and selflessness must be the rule of life. Socrates is right: "The shortest and surest way to live with honor in the world is to be in reality what we appear to be." Most people are glad to follow pastoral leaders who demonstrate rocklike fidelity to Christ.

4. No Room for Elitism

Men and women of God for the new century must renounce elitism of every kind. Throughout Nazarene history, our preachers have warned against pride of grace, race, face, place, and lace. But sly forms of egotism of academic prowess are sometimes allowed or even encouraged these days. I mean students must die out to spiritual conceit and intellectual haughtiness. God loves and uses the humble.

5. Support

Men and women of God for the new century must grasp economic realities. Facts about student loans, bivocational-ism, and income supplement must be thoroughly under-stood. There is a strength we can cherish in the fact that our denominational budget system strongly encourages a pastor to good management of congregational finance, a strength that carries over to personal finance.

However, we must also recognize the fact that heavy eco-nomic burdens of many churches are being carried on the spouse's shoulders. Pressing financial issues may compel our denomination to institute resourceful new approaches to clergy compensation and placement procedures.

6. Outreach

Men and women of God for the new century must give priority to mission and outreach. They must be trained in cross-cultural skills so they can effectively share the gospel with everyone, including immigrants and secularists. Such an emphasis on the Master's mandate will refocus our mis-sion, increase our membership, and bring great satisfaction to the preacher.

The components of becoming missional include church planting, revivals, church growth, evangelism, church health, witnessing, discipleship, assimilation, and nurture. Our graduates must be awed by the fact that our Lord wants everyone saved.

7. Renewal

Men and women of God for the new century must be-come pacesetters of renewal. The world and church need a revolutionary spiritual awakening. We must have it. The re-newal for which I intercede is summarized in two sentences from John Gardner: "Institutions are renewed by individuals who refuse to be satisfied with the outer husks of things.

And self-renewal requires somewhat the same impatience with empty forms."

Our students must be taught to establish and maintain spiritually vigorous churches where they serve healthy doses of faith, hope, and mercy. They must also learn to stir up holy fires in dying churches. They must be taught to use God's timeless renewal remedies such as worship, prayer, Scripture saturation, fasting, and personal piety. The world is ripe for spiritual reformation, maybe even ready for a prophet from among our students to point us all to God.

8. Ethnic and Urban Focus

Men and women of God for the new century must be skilled in urban and ethnic communication and evangelism. Social scientists tell us that soon one child in three in the United States will be from a Hispanic or non-Anglo background. To reach underevangelized groups, we must recruit and train more ethnic pastors, especially Hispanic, African-Americans, Native Americans, and Asians. At the same time, Anglo students must be shown how to respond to this challenge, which is too big for any ethnic group to accomplish by itself.

9. User-Friendly Churches

Men and women of God for the new century must develop user-friendly churches. Many who need the gospel will never be attracted by pious mumbo jumbo, obscure theological jargon, religious pop psychology, or archaic procedures. Preachers must recognize there is a momentous difference between a layperson's tolerance and wholehearted endorsement of the pastor's ministry. For the layperson, the contrast is like eating oatmeal to keep alive or feasting on steak and lobster. Seeking some kind of ministry that is relevant to life, laypersons vote on these issues with intensity of involvement, attendance, and giving. An accurate exegesis of these needs must be branded into every student's perception of ministry.

10. Connection to Life

Men and women of God for the new century must connect theology to life. Doctrine must be understandable and incarnated on Main Street. Neutrality never wins wars and does not work well in preparation for ministry classrooms. A life-throbbing link must be forged between theology and ministry. While I preached in an African-American church, a brother helped me by shouting, "Make it plain, Brother. Make it plain." That's the preacher's task in every generation and in every setting.

Fervor for truth, righteousness, and morality must be evident and emphasized in every classroom. Truth we know about God, Jesus Christ, and the Holy Spirit, assurance of resurrection faith, plus realities about hope and love must be connected with intensity and affection to the everyday world where people live, work, and die.

11. New Testament Lifestyle

Men and women of God for the new century must be challenged to live a radical New Testament lifestyle even though nothing in the culture encourages such a commitment. Students must learn to live with downward mobility in a world dominated by upward mobility. Students must be prepared to tackle tough assignments so they thoroughly transform those situations into great missional churches. Missional ministry must be viewed as an adventure worth any sacrifice.

SUMMARY—MISSIONAL COMMITMENTS

I pray that with our hearts we will hear so many congregations crying for competent servant pastors to lead them. As students and teachers, I hope we are compelled by a visionary pursuit to be all we can be, to be all our founders intended, and to be all the church needs us to be.

A veteran pastor had just finished dedicating a child. After solemnly charging her parents to nurture the child, he said to the sleeping infant, "My dear one, I have no idea where life will take you, but I know our Lord will go with you wherever you go." That is the bottom-line confidence that God will help the church prepare men and women of God who will go to missional assignments and achieve more for Him than anyone ever dreamed they could.

Let's pray for missional leaders to be called by the Spirit of God to make every community a mission station, every church a mission outpost, and every pastor a missionary.

Let's ask the Lord to help the ministry shapers prepare women and men of God to match our mission.

———○———

The missionary church
keeps its members living
the Christian message of love
by drawing them into missionary lives
based on the Great Commission
and the Great Commandment.

—Claude E. Payne
Reclaiming the Great Commission

———○———

9

THE INCREDIBLE POSSIBILITIES BEFORE US

Bill M. Sullivan

GOD IS STIRRING the Nazarene missionary spirit to respond to pressing spiritual needs of Canada and the United States. When the Board of General Superintendents declared Canada and the United States to be mission fields, surprising responses started happening at once. That decision resonated with what a faithful intercessor said was an answer to her prayers.

"What church culture people see as evidence of success matters little to pre-Christians."

The declaration of our leaders fits our times well. Their call to become more missional in the United States and Canada comes at a time when masses of modern people are starting to see that stuff and technology never make good on their promises. One hint of bad news in their physicians' offices undermines decades of secular values. Many serious Christian thinkers advise that secular people are increasingly searching for meaning, purpose, love, self-worth, and a sense of transcendence. New Age books and secular magazines discussing personal spirituality can be found in every bookstore and attract readers by the thousands. At the same time, many leaders of local congregations feel uncomfortable with the powerful, hard-to-explain, attractive, and hard-to-control presence of God. As a result, they try to lead congregations to better programs and greater efficiency when the world seems to be looking for God. On this issue Reggie McNeal warns: "What church culture people see as evidence of success matters little to pre-Christians. . . . Today's church service had better get God up front, center stage, and in a hurry, or pre-Christians will not take the church seriously as a source of spiritual help." The challenge for every missional church is to help spiritually hungry people experience the God of the Bible, as seen in Jesus Christ.

Within a matter of months after the announcement was made by the general superintendents, missionaries to Canada and the United States were recruited and commissioned by the General Board. Districts started creative missional initiatives; examples include New England, Chicago Central, West Texas, South Carolina, and Washington Districts.

The New England District has refocused their geographical zones into missional groupings so pastors and congregations pray and plan together to plant new churches in their area of the district; a district missionary has been named to lead the charge to reopen closed historic old-line churches in Vermont and New Hampshire.

Chicago Central has a five-point missional plan with a goal of starting 100 new works by 2010, giving special attention to 77 specific Chicago neighborhoods.

South Carolina has implemented a two-pronged missional plan to plant NewStart churches sponsored by local congregations and groups of churches and also to plant 40 Hope in Christ Centers across the state where a compassion ministry center will provide the facility for a new church.

West Texas District is working a splendid plan to plant Hispanic churches in smaller towns across their rural areas; a lead church is being developed around small groups in Lubbock, which will serve as a model and as a resource center for other churches. West Texas is also giving renewed emphasis called Mission 820 to its inner-city ministry in Fort Worth.

The Washington District has a plan to use day cares to start urban churches and to use volunteer missionaries to the city to establish new works and to strengthen existing churches.

Dialogue, discussions, debates, prayer, and sermons on the idea are still going on. Some call all this a spiritual revolution.

Fifteen hundred or more people gathered for the Gateway Missional Conference in Olathe, Kansas, in October 2000. What a conference it was—an epic milestone that attenders will remember for years. This conference was a missional conference—that is much more than a multicultural conference. Its main focus was on building awareness and finding strategies for meeting nearby missional opportunities in Canada and the United States.

Conferees Are Ready

Young people ready to commit their futures to be missionaries in the United States and Canada attended.

I believe our people have a missionary spirit they want to express in commitment and hope that will impact the Church of the Nazarene in the United States and Canada like nothing else has ever done in our denomination's history.

Immigrants from many countries of the world came because, like the apostle Paul, their heart's desire is to see people from their homeland saved.

Burdened Nazarenes who recognize the secularization of Canada and the United States and are willing to do primary evangelism came.

Pastors and lay leaders seeking the most effective strategies for planting strong new churches attended the conference too.

Most all of us attended the conference to better understand culture and what really matters to secularists.

The preaching, the singing, the workshops, even the breaks fairly crackled with a missionary spirit. I believe our people have a missionary spirit they want to express in commitment and hope that will impact the Church of the Nazarene in the United States and Canada like nothing else has ever done in our denomination's history.

Urgent Need for Missional Ministry

Consider these symptoms of spiritual decline. We are nations

> —that forbid religious expression at public gatherings
> —whose schools teach as though God does not exist
> —where Sunday School attendance has plummeted and biblical illiteracy skyrocketed
> —where people's religious claims make no difference in their daily lives
> —where millions have no Christian memory
> —where the number of churches per population is less than half of what it was 100 years ago
> —where people are absorbed in personal interests and have little or no time for God or religion

Such nations can no longer call themselves Christian nations. Though these countries may be economically and educationally developed, they are no more spiritually developed than Africa or Asia. Such countries are mission fields needing the gospel to be communicated in words they understand through competent witnesses who are authentically Christian.

WHAT A NEEDY MISSION FIELD WE LIVE IN!

What a mission field stands at the door of our churches. The size of our opportunity and the magnitude of our responsibility are hard to comprehend. I was spiritually stretched by an article, "What a Mission Field!" that appeared in a recent issue of *GROW* magazine. Inspired by Keith Wright's annual report to the Kansas City District, the article written by Mark Graham communicated a soul burden for mission. Let me share from it extensively:

Does the idea of a mission field create imagery of villages far away with colorful persons speaking strange languages with even stranger customs? Or maybe the concept of a mission field makes you think of missionaries—doctors, nurses, preachers, farmers, and others—and how they take cups of cold water and the gospel to men, women, boys and girls in distant places you can't even pronounce.

Certainly Jesus calls us to make disciples of all nations, and the Church of the Nazarene does this as well as any denomination on earth. With 735 missionaries and volunteers serving in 135 areas, our denomination continues to plant congregations and grow at a healthy pace around the world. By its commitment to taking the gospel to places beyond our borders Nazarenes have shown they truly are a missionary-minded people.

But what about closer to home? What about the mission field of your own city, suburb, or town? You don't have to take a series of vaccinations. You don't even have to pack your bags. The mission field is at your doorstep. There are people nearby who hunger and thirst for a better life—here and in the hereafter. But they will only find it if persons like you and me are willing to open our eyes and our hearts to respond.

It will require that we learn how they think and what they consider important. We will have to study secular culture like missionaries study customs and practices of people they want to win. But they are our neighbors.

169.9 Million Prospects

Where are these mission fields? While driving to church next Sunday morning, take a few extra minutes to cruise your neighborhood. You'll probably notice a lot of people doing things other than going to church. Sure—there are some who now worship on Friday evenings or Saturdays, but the fact that you see people heading for the lake, sporting events, or just mowing the yard on Sunday mornings is a pretty good indication that such folks aren't regular church-goers. Many of them have no idea what the church really is or what Christ could do in their lives.

About 15 percent (42.5 million people) of the United States do not claim to be part of the Christian religion. The 1990 Census of Religious Bodies tells us that about 45 percent (127.4 million) are not claimed by any Christian group. According to George Gallup, about 60 percent (169.9 million) do not claim to have attended church recently. The unreached, unchurched millions—what a mission field!

178.6 Million Urban Dwellers

Our cities or "urban areas," as the United States Census Bureau prefers to call communities of 50,000 or greater, are filled with people who need the Lord. Currently, there are 47 metropolitan statistical areas in the United States with at least 1,000,000 inhabitants. Between 1998 and 2003, urbanized areas in the United States are expected to grow by 7 million people to 178.6 million (63 percent of the population). Thousands of urban areas need us to return or go to them for the first time with the Good News. Cities—what a mission field!

16.6 Million Single-Parent Families

Divorce has created a new and particularly needy demographic in our nation—single-parent families. Most such families are headed by women who generally have a difficult task maintaining households with limited time and income. Approximately 23 percent of United States families (16.6 million) are headed by single parents. As of 1998 there were 16.6 million children under the age of 18 in these families. A church in my community is currently providing a special ministry to a group of single-parent mothers. Services range from car repair to assistance with managing personal finances. Other ministries, such as tutoring or after-school care, could be provided for these children. Single-parent families—what a mission field!

40.6 Million Children

Then there are the children. Between the years of 1998 and 2003, the number of children between the ages of 5 and 14 in the United States will grow by 1.5 million to 40.6 million. Beyond the numbers are the problems of children—like the school shootings. According to church researchers, 80 percent of all conversions to Christianity take place between the ages of 5 and 15. Some forward-thinking churches have started whole new ministries for children, some have even restarted bus ministries that fell dormant in the 1970s. How much heartache and related problems could be avoided if we would make a special effort to reach the boys and girls of our communities? Children—what a mission field!

Other Next-Door Mission Fields

There are other groups we could mention for which getting the actual statistics are trickier, but they represent sizable groups all the same. Consider those in the United States who are moving to rural settings—some to work from home on their computers and others as retirees. What a mission field!

Think of the number of apartment dwellers in your community. What a mission field!

Or how about visitors to your church? Research indicates that the number of people who visit a church during a year will generally equal that church's average attendance. Visitors—what a mission field!

We could list many other examples, but you get the picture. The fields are full and they are ripe. The harvest is waiting for the gathering. God has given us the command to go and make disciples. Let's spend more time focusing on ministry to those who need the Lord nearby.

The U.S.A. and Canada—what a mission field!

NEW CHURCHES MAKE US MISSIONAL

Our denomination has come to realize in the last few years that starting strong new churches is among the most effective strategies for winning secular people. Our pastors and lay leaders are responding to the prophetic words from Kevin W. Mannoia: "God is calling His body, the Church, to come off the mountain of our own comfort zone and enter the valley where the battle is hot. He wants us to declare His kingdom to the world. There is no more effective way to do so than to start new churches."

And we want to start new churches the right way so they thrive and win thousands of people.

Think large and small at the same time. Westminster Church of the Nazarene in Denver is a large church. Its Sunday morning worship attendance is about 700. It has great property and facilities. Many people have come to Christ as a result of that church. There are students at Nazarene universities from that church, and there has been a steady stream of students from the Westminster church involved in district and general church activities for many years.

But I remember when the Westminster church was a fledgling little congregation meeting in the living room of a concrete block house. You see, I was the founding pastor of that church, and I remember when it was one of those "poor little church starts" we disdain because of their weakness and smallness.

We often forget that every strong church was once a small, struggling group of Christians trying to grow into a larger church, secure property, and construct a sanctuary and educational space.

Grove City church near Columbus, Ohio, started even more recently than the Westminster church. Believe me—it didn't start off 3,000 strong. It had to go through those meager beginning days of birth and development.

In fact, most, if not all, churches begin small and go through a period of struggling and trying to keep their head above water. Like people, churches experience birth, childhood, and maturity.

There are scores of new, small, struggling churches today that 20 years from now will be flagship churches of the denomination. Recently I preached at the organization of a brand-new church sponsored by the Coeur d'Alene, Idaho, church on the Northwest District. It is a fine group of Christians. They have a wonderful young pastor and wife, several strong laypersons, great music, and enough enthusiasm to fill a football stadium. They have a very bright future, but right now it is "hand-to-mouth" time. They face many challenges, and like other churches, they will just have to work their way through them.

It is so important for Nazarenes to accept "the day of small things" in these new churches. True, many churches never grow out of the struggling stage. But if we avoid starting new churches because many of them never become what we hoped they would be, we will never have the Grove Cities, the Westminsters, or the Phoenix CrossRoads.

Churches are like people. They experience birth, infancy, childhood, old age, and death. Yes, death. Did you know over 5,000 Nazarene churches have already died and been buried in our 92-year history?

Birthing new churches is essential to replace the ones

that die. Every church should be involved to some degree in helping start another church that will replace them when they are gone. The truth is, there are many congregations that need to start a new church right now to replace themselves, because they will be gone in a few years. That may sound absurd, but if we care about the future, we will accept reality and plan for the inevitable.

Important as this is, there is an even more important reason for starting new churches—evangelism. Did you know starting new churches is the most effective method of evangelism the Church has ever found?

Twenty years ago when I came to Kansas City to be director of evangelism, the New York District had 4,580 members. Soon afterward, they elected a district superintendent by the name of Dallas Mucci. Dal and I were involved in a meeting in Kansas City just about the time he was elected. As I recall, we teased him about becoming a district superintendent. Truthfully, we felt a little sorry for him going to such a small and difficult district.

But Dal began starting churches. Everywhere, and every way he could, he started new churches. Across 20 years, he never took a "breather" to catch up on all of the outstanding obligations new churches produce. He just kept on starting new churches.

When he began, there were 57 churches and missions on the New York District. Today, there are 139. Membership is now twice what it was in 1980. Without all of the new churches, the New York District would only have 6,500 members today instead of its present 10,848.

If the church in the United States had continued starting as many new churches per decade as it did in the 1920s, 1930s, 1940s, and 1950s, we would now have over 7,500 churches in the United States and a membership nearing 900,000. And instead of winning 30,000 new Nazarenes per year, as we do now, we would be winning 44,000 new Nazarenes each year. Those extra 14,000 people are a tremendous evangelistic difference.

The mission of the Church of the Nazarene is to win people to Christ and the church. The most effective way to do that is to start new churches. The more churches we start, the more people we will win to Christ and the church.

Recently, at the Intermediate Church Initiative Conference in Indianapolis, Leith Anderson spoke to us. He is the pastor of the Wooddale Church—a megachurch near Minneapolis. He is also a well-known author of several books, including *A Church for the 21st Century*. He was elected president of Denver Seminary but declined, choosing rather to remain a pastor. I mention this about him because I want you to know his leadership capabilities are extensive.

After the session, in the midst of our conversation, right out of the blue he said to me, "I want you to know I am passionate about starting new churches. Our congregation used to start a new church every two years, but we feel so strongly about it we are now starting two churches every year."

As we talked about the number of churches that are dying and how few new churches are being started each year, he made this remarkable statement: "The 21st century belongs to the denomination that starts new churches."

Why shouldn't the 21st century belong to this Holiness denomination called the Church of the Nazarene?

We used to start 150 new churches each year. Now we start less than 50 each year. We have many more churches now, and much more money, than we had when we were starting 150 new churches a year. Of course, it costs more money to start a new church today than it used to require, but our resources are far greater now than they used to be.

I challenge the Church of the Nazarene in the United States and Canada to make starting new churches the number one priority—starting right now.

Since the United States and Canada are now mission fields, let's do what Nazarene missionaries do on foreign mission fields—let's start new churches. That's the reason our fastest growing mission fields are experiencing such exciting expansion—they are starting new churches.

We can see phenomenal growth in the United States and Canada if local churches will commit themselves to sponsoring new congregations. Every local church can become involved in sponsoring a new church, either by themselves or in cooperation with other churches. Even a group of small churches can sponsor a new congregation on their zone or in their county.

If every church over 250 would sponsor a new church every 5 years—

If churches between 100 and 250 would join in groups of three and sponsor a new church every 10 years—

If churches under 100 would join in groups of 10 and sponsor a new church every 10 years—

That would result in 1,800 new churches per decade. We would net 1,300 churches per decade, and in 40 years we would have over 10,000 churches and well over a million members. In addition, we would have won 2 million new Nazarenes to Christ and the church.

In the 40-year period from 1920 to 1960, we started 5,810 churches. We did it then with less than half the resources we have now.

We can do it again. All that is required is
- a red-hot holy fire in our hearts
- an absolutely dependent faith in the power of God
- and bulldog tenacity to see the job through

Let's go from reading the incredible challenges found on every page of this book with one passionate commitment—

Start new churches!
Start new churches!
Start new churches!